SHINING THE LIGHT

THE TRUTH ABOUT
ETs • SECRET GOVERNMENT • ALIEN BASES
THE BATTLE BEGINS!

LIGHT TECHNOLOGY RESEARCH

SHINING THE LIGHT

THE TRUTH ABOUT
- ETs
- Secret Government
- Alien Bases

The Battle Begins

Light Technology
Research

Cover art by
Robert Lewis Arnold
Balance

ISBN 0-929385-66-7

Published by
Light Technology Publishing
P.O. Box 1526
Sedona, AZ 86339

Printed by

**MISSION
POSSIBLE**
Commercial
Printing

P.O. Box 1495
Sedona, AZ 86339

Preface

Welcome to our latest Adventure in Consciousness! We are doing something that hasn't been done before — going from one dimension to another while living in the physical body during the change in state. Add to that challenge the turmoil caused by the controlling, manipulating shadow government with their ET allies and space-age technology — with all of us on a planet that needs to take care of her own needs as she goes through her transformation, and we are guaranteed some interesting possible and probable experiences ahead. *USA Today* quoted Rep. Jim Nussle, R-Iowa, in the context of the GOP takeover of the House as saying, "It's like building a rocket ship while it's taking off." That has some of the flavor of what humanity is going through now as we move beyond the limitations of the third dimension.

This book documents flying craft, both Earth and off-Earth, and the workings of the shadow government and their ET allies through pictures, descriptions of people's experiences and information from channeled entities to "Shine the Light" on what is really going on here and now as well as there and then.

It is the end times. As Jehovah says, "The Battle Begins" between the forces of Light and the forces of darkness.

Stay tuned for further installments, both in the *Sedona Journal of Emergence*, in which much of this material has previously been printed, and in future *Shining the Light* books.

O'Ryin Swanson
Publisher

Tom Dongo is an author and UFO researcher who lives in Sedona, Arizona. His intuitive ability to be at the right place at the right time to see and photograph off-world flying craft and Secret Governmment timeships, his growing network of friends and fellow researchers and the clear, concise and colorful way he writes about what he sees, hears and experiences have made him a valuable contributor both to the *Sedona Journal of Emergence* and to this book.

Tom has a long metaphysical history: from being a channel, to teaching channeling, to remote viewing. His present focus, however, is on bringing to humanity the documentation and proof of the existence of craft and beings from other worlds, other civilizations, other dimensions in a manner acceptable to all, whatever their present belief systems may be.

Tom can be reached at P.O. Box 2571, Sedona, AZ, 86339.

Other books by Tom Dongo
Published by Hummingbird Publishing

THE MYSTERY OF SEDONA Series:
Book One, *The Mystery of Sedona*
Book Two, *The Alien Tide*
Book Three, *The Quest*

Unseen Beings, Unseen Worlds

Arthur Fanning was born and raised in Providence, Rhode Island. He attended the University of Rhode Island, receiving a B.S. degree in agriculture. After graduation, he entered the U.S. Marine Corps in the officer candidate program. Upon graduation he earned his navy wings at Pensacola Naval Air Station in Florida. From 1968 to 1969 he was a marine helicopter pilot in Vietnam.

Arthur had many experiences as a little child, leaving his body and talking with beings in the stars at night. As a medivac pilot in Vietnam, the real nature of these experiences began to reveal themselves to him as a guiding and guarding force that all beings share.

In 1986 he had what he calls the "Big One" of his spiritual awakening. An entity appeared over his bed while Arthur was still awake. Arthur's body lifted off the bed, bent in half, straightened out horizontally, and then laid back down, all in less than two seconds. There was no pain involved, nor was it frightening. Arthur says, "It just happened. It felt like white electricity."

Since then, Arthur has been channeling and working with the entity that appeared to him above his bed —Jehovah/YHWH. His first book, *Simon*, was his first attempt to explain some of the phenomena he has experienced in his spiritual awakening. The material was excerpted from both his physical life and his dreaming life. The second book, *Soul, Evolution, Father* was dictated through him by Jehovah.

Arthur Fanning lives with his wife Cheryl and may be contacted for channeling and healing appointments at P.O. Box 684, Cornville, AZ 86325.

Jehovah/YHWH is part of a great group of beings from another universe who created and are responsible for maintaining this part of the galaxy. His sense of adventure and his great love, wisdom and compassion for humanity radiate through the energy and words of his channeling through Arthur.

Other books by Arthur Fanning
Published by Light Technology Publishing

Simon
Soul, Evolution, Father

Robert Shapiro is a man who has grown up with the experience of extra-terrestrial contact. From age twelve he has had a series of personal UFO contacts. Throughout his life there have been communication with beings from several star systems and dimensions. The development of his career and life-style has come as a direct result of this communication. Robert has been a professional channel for over 15 years, and although he can channel almost anyone or anything with an exceptionally clear and profound connection, he most often channels Zoosh, who describes himself below. Robert's great contribution to an understanding of the history and purpose of humanity is his epochal work, *The Explorer Race,* and he is one of several channels featured in *Sedona Vortex Guidebook.* When he is not channeling, Robert is a shaman and spiritual teacher in his own right. He lives with his wife Nancy in Sedona, Arizona. He is available for personal appointments and can be reached at (602) 282-5883; P.O. Box 2849, Sedona, AZ 86339.

Zoosh ensouled the first planet that humanity experienced as souls and he has been with us ever since, for "about a trillion years." He is witty, wise and compassionate. He says about himself, "It has been my job and my purpose in life to follow the birth of your souls on your journey to recreating the universe. My job is to be your companion, your guide, occasionally your entertainer. I have to nurture that sense of mystery — it's not as if you're going to have it forever.

"It is my job to help you get there, to help you to understand your experience and to observe everything. And, in time, to remind you of the everything you are in one of my many guises."

Other books by Robert Shapiro
Published by Light Technology Publishing

The Explorer Race
Sedona Vortex Guidebook

Contents

SHINING THE LIGHT

THE TRUTH ABOUT

- ETs
- Secret Government
- Alien Bases

The Battle Begins

Light Technology
Research

UFO Crash in Sedona?

by Tom Dongo
July 25, 1994

During the Memorial Day weekend of May 28-30, 1994, an event of national significance occurred near Sedona, Arizona. The information I have gathered points to several probabilities. I think what occurred was either the crash of a UFO, a major landing of a UFO, the downing of a jet fighter by a UFO or vice versa, or something else which may have been a combination of any of the above.

A friend in Air Force Intelligence (generally known as O.S.I.) once said to me that in an intelligence investigation if as few as two circumstantial events point directly to a separate probable event, then the separate event is assumed as fact and the investigation proceeds from there. That is the point I have arrived at here. All evidence, both direct and circumstantial, points to the landing, crash or otherwise, of an airborne object of extreme interest to the U.S. military and our national government. Quoting from a letter to a Cottonwood, Arizona, UFO researcher from a Nevada private investigator who had knowledge of the details of an event during its occurrence: "I just happen to think that you might be sitting on top of the hottest opportunity to expose a covert government operation that's ever come along. This has the possibility of becoming the most definitive exposé ever to surface revealing government and ET-related activities. The Roswell incident [the Roswell, New Mexico UFO crash of 1947] could be a second-rate story compared to this." In a few sentences I think that statement accurately sums up the Sedona area Memorial Day weekend series of occurrences.

Related incidents and sightings point to the days between May 25 and June 2 as being the key period. I am going to present in chronological order this information I have gathered and my own conclusions. Because there was nowhere to go externally for answers to the puzzling sightings and experiences being reported, other sources of information were sought. Therefore, following the accounts I have written about these occurrences are channeled viewpoints from trusted sources. I purposely and intentionally did not and do not want to know what the channels reported, as I did not want it to influence my writing and research in any way. So what I have written is totally separate from the channeled material and is presented from a rather clinical research perspective.

The strange events of the 1994 Memorial Day weekend began for me personally in this manner: About 11:00 a.m. on Sunday, May 29, I was driving northeast in the left lane on highway 89A entering Sedona when a tractor-trailer rig passed me in the right lane — the slow lane. The truck was going about ten miles an hour over the posted 40 mph speed limit. The cab itself was ordinary and a drab white color. But the flatbed trailer it was pulling drew my attention. Being a researcher of the unusual and one who is naturally curious anyway, I look at and take note of anything out of the ordinary. When the white cab passed me, I got a good look at the flatbed it was hauling. What was extremely odd about it was the cover material over the load. I had never seen anything like it. It was a thick olive-drab plastic, stretched so tight that it looked like Saran Wrap stretched over a platter of cut-up vegetables. The plastic was the same color and thickness as a Vietnam body bag once so often shown on television. There was one round object standing upright in the center of the load that was about four feet high and appeared to be hollow. It was about 30 inches in diameter and looked quite sharp, similar to a length of steel pipe.

The plastic must have been extremely strong, as it was not torn by the edges of this round object. When truckers cover a flatbed load they usually use inexpensive, clear plastic tarpaulins or plain or waterproof canvas tarps. When the odd flatbed passed me I had not yet heard any current reports of strange sightings in the Sedona area. The highly unusual tarp, however, stuck in my mind. Shortly after I got home came a flood of information from many sources. The town was beginning to buzz with strange stories. Too much was happening too fast to be the work of a few paranoid or intentional rumor-makers.

There was an urgent phone message to call a woman friend who

The Secret at SEDONA – 29 May 1994

Figure 1.   Courtesy Miller Johnson

is a UFO investigator in Cottonwood. Cottonwood is a city of about 6,000 fifteen miles southwest of Sedona. I returned her call that afternoon of the 29th. As soon as she picked up the phone she exclaimed, "Do you know what is happening around here?!" She was so excited that I was instantly alerted and at the same time a little miffed that I didn't know what "it" was. (I am usually the first one around here to hear dramatic news of any kind.) Turns out she had been investigating the stories for two days. She continued with startling news of dozens of military helicopters landing on the ground in Cornville; FBI all over Sedona; dead, possibly mutilated cattle found on House Mountain; UFOs flying over Cottonwood daytime and nighttime; and a group of mountain bikers being stopped and turned back at gunpoint near the mouth of Secret Canyon by the U.S. military with M-16 assault rifles. She went on to say that Senators Dole and Mitchell had been seen in Sedona a week before all this unusual activity began. I was not expecting such an avalanche of stimulating news and was a bit speechless at first. I thanked her for calling me, and we agreed to stay in close contact to share information and see what else might develop in the meantime.

While I stood there trying to integrate this bewildering information and make some sense of it, the phone rang. The call was from a woman in Tucson, also a UFO researcher, who exclaimed in a concerned, agitated tone, "Tom, what the hell is going on in Sedona?

I just got a call from a friend in the U.S. Senate. I was told that there was some sort of an incident, maybe involving a UFO, near Sedona and that the military was preparing to seal off all routes into and out of Sedona. What's going on?" My Tucson friend, who knew nothing of the other incidents being reported in the Sedona area, could not have been influenced by those stories. I asked her if her Senate friend knew what had happened here. She replied that her friend might have known, but didn't tell her. I got the impression that her friend wanted to leak information but was afraid to be more specific. It could be, I thought, that her friend in the Senate was, like everyone else, just trying to find out what was going on.

My investigator/researcher brain shifted into high gear as I began to smell a UFO crash. I have been near this sort of thing before. I knew the signs. And I knew I had to move fast before the trail got cold. In the UFO business, hours or days can mean the difference between a major event or a cold, unverifiable rumor. I started calling people on the phone and asking lots of questions. One thing quickly led to another, and I had more and more pieces of the puzzle. At the time I was also all too well aware of the military's quick-recovery teams. These teams are stationed around the country and can be mobilized and at the site of a UFO crash in a matter of hours. When one of these teams arrives at a crash site, they clean up the site so well that it is generally restored to its original condition.

I am asked sometimes how a UFO can possibly crash, given their technology. For one thing, it's evident that they occasionally do have mechanical problems, sometimes with disastrous results, such as the presently well-published UFO crashes at Aztec, New Mexico; Roswell, New Mexico; and Kecksburg, Pennsylvania. I have also seen on videotape a Russian Air Force colonel (in uniform) vehemently telling an American UFO researcher that both the U.S. and the Russians have particle-beam weapons fully capable of shooting down an alien spaceship. The Russian colonel demonstrated, on camera, a small version of their beam weapon. It was impressive. He said the Americans have an operative beam weapon that is far more destructive than the one they have. A close associate and friend of mine who is an American Air Force colonel says he watched as one of these U.S. beam weapons was being readied for firing, although he did not see it in operation.

The question is, are they shooting back? I think so, because the Russian colonel said that in a Soviet effort to collect a UFO, three of their most advanced M.I.G. fighters were shot down by UFOs. He says they now have a hands-off policy toward UFOs.

Speed, prudence and caution are my guidelines, because I know what I might be dealing with. During the course of my investigation a man told me that he had heard that several roads out in the desert had been blocked by military vehicles. I had no way to verify this report/rumor, but what gave it a measure of credibility was that I heard the rumor before anyone else knew what the Tucson woman had told me. I was the first local person to hear of the possibility of Sedona being sealed off.

It seems that a hornet's nest of UFO and paranormal-type activity was stirred up that Memorial Day weekend. I am certain that most, if not all of it, was directly connected even though some of the reports seemed to be unrelated. I say that because all of what I narrate here occurred during a period of about ten days, with Memorial Day the focus. Those events are as follows, as close as I could put them in chronological order.

On May 29 at 8:23 p.m. a red-ringed UFO was seen moving in unusual aerial patterns in the eastern sky as seen from Cottonwood. This UFO was watched by four adults and was described as glowing and pulsating. Then two smaller, white-glowing objects flew directly over the four witnesses at a high rate of speed. One UFO was flying straight, but the other was erratic, as though it were having some sort of control problem. Both white UFOs then disappeared into a cloud. The red-ringed object had also moved out of sight. That same evening at 10:22 p.m. — again from Cottonwood — nine adult witnesses observed two red-ringed UFOs flying seemingly in a search pattern for one and one-half hours in the direction of House Mountain. House Mountain lies halfway between Sedona and Cottonwood and is adjacent to the small settlements of Cornville and Page Springs. During the course of my investigation several people had asked, "How come all this stuff didn't appear in the local newspapers?" My answer was that the mainstream media ignore UFO activity and stories these days, and even if somebody dragged a spaceship into town behind their pickup, newspapers probably wouldn't report it.

In a separate sighting that Sunday night, four adults watched two orange balls of light fly at high altitude over Cottonwood and disappear to the southwest over Mingus Mountain. This was at 11:45 p.m. I might add here that the "UFOs" the U.S. government has been flying at the supersecret Area 51 base 100 miles north of Las Vegas in almost every instance glow a bright orange color. It seems that these UFOs have either been constructed with alien help or been "back engineered," meaning built or reconstructed by salvaging a

Figure 2. House Mountain from the south.

crashed (or donated) alien craft. These craft, it seems, are being flown by U.S. military personnel or are a joint venture by U.S. and alien pilots. I have an excellent nighttime color photo taken by a California physicist of one of these very same Area 51 craft. Were these orange balls of light that were flying over Cottonwood U.S. government craft? I think they were. Either that or the same ships being flown by aliens.

Also on May 29, a Cottonwood man and his wife watched a single glowing orange object slowly fly over Cottonwood at an altitude of approximately 6000 feet. They remarked that the UFO was very bright orange and moved south at a leisurely speed. At 9:30 p.m. on the same night the red-ringed UFOs were again seen, this time near House Mountain, which is 5127 feet high from a base elevation of about 4000 feet. It is an expansive, rather rounded and unpopulated desert mountain with a base circumference of approximately ten miles. That same evening, also at 9:30 p.m., a dark UFO "the size of a football field" with two blinking lights on either end flew slowly east between House Mountain and Camp Verde. Witnesses said this object flew in a slow, sweeping motion, and while it was in view two red-glowing UFOs were seen hovering far above the enormous dark UFO. This lasted for over 40 minutes before the three objects disappeared in the distance. The next day (May 30) two black military helicopters were seen flying around the same area

Figure 3.   House Mountain from the west.

where the one large and two smaller UFOs had been seen the night before.

During the entire three-day Memorial Day weekend, U.S. Apache and Cobra attack helicopters were flying at low altitude, particularly in the Sedona area. They were flying, patrol fashion, in groups of two to six. At one point five Apache helicopters flew in a line south to north over Sedona at a height of 300 feet or less. These are loud, powerful helicopters. I spoke to an ex-military man who told me that some of the helicopters he saw over Sedona that weekend were combat-ready, with loaded rocket launchers. Four of these helicopters flew over me and were indeed equipped with loaded rocket launchers and, in my opinion, seemed to be looking for something to shoot at.

Again that Sunday holiday, a group of four women UFO researchers who had been noticing the odd activity around House Mountain decided to go there to investigate. They had driven along the road on the south and west sides of the mountain and had seen nothing unusual. Deciding to return to Cottonwood in early afternoon, they were near Cornville when two black cars came racing up behind them at a high rate of speed. Both approaching cars, the women said, were shiny black, new, and each had short antennas sticking out both the driver's and the passenger's side windows. One black car passed the four women and pulled in front — close. The women were now boxed in between the two black cars, both driven by men and displaying black Arizona license plates with white numerals. Black Arizona plates are unusual; they are normally maroon with white numerals. The two black cars followed the women researchers for about five minutes; then the car following them pulled out and passed. Both cars then accelerated down the narrow highway. The women estimated that the two cars were going over 80 mph as they sped out of sight on the narrow, curving rural highway.

The women, again curious and thinking they were in the clear, went back to House Mountain to look around some more. They turned off on unpaved National Forest Road 120, which leads into a remote area where several dead cattle had been found the day before by a local man. He said the cattle may have been mutilated UFO style, but not being an expert in that field, he could not be sure. On one long, open section of 120 were the imprints of a wide-tracked vehicle. The tracks went off into the desert, coming to an end behind an area with thick brush. In itself this was odd because there was no evidence of work being done on the gravel road by maintenance crews. Ranchers do not use tracked vehicles in this area. They almost exclusively use four-wheel-drive or two-wheel-drive pickup trucks.

The four women then made a wide loop around House Mountain, taking photos as they went. They continued on State Highway 179 into the Village of Oak Creek, then on into Sedona, turning left onto State Route 89A to return to Cottonwood. As the women were passing the Sedona city limits, two black military helicopters appeared out of nowhere and began pacing them. The helicopters followed them fifteen miles, all the way to Cottonwood. They even followed them along the winding back roads to the home of one of the women. This activity was witnessed by the husband of one of the women. He remarked that from his higher vantage point it was obvious that these two black multimillion-dollar military helicopters had been following them. The question is, why? Did the four women get too close to something they were not supposed to see? All of the photographs taken by the women that afternoon came out black. Photos on that same roll of 35-mm film taken several days before developed normally. This has happened before around here during UFO activity. It takes strong radiation to black out a roll of film like that. In one other case I know of similar to the four women's experience, it was obvious that some sort of device was "beamed" toward the photographer. The photographer in the second case was shooting photos of a ball of white light hovering near her in the open desert near Sedona.

That same day, again on Sunday, May 29, a Cornville man driving east on rural route 119 between Cornville and McGuireville saw in the distance over a dozen military helicopters on the ground. This report says that the man counted seventeen helicopters sitting on a high mesa between House Mountain and McGuireville. This would have been about two air miles from where the four women researchers were that day when photographing and tracking imprints of a large, tracked vehicle and subsequently followed by two military helicopters. It seems those seventeen helicopters were positioned in a staging area ready to move at a moment's notice to a nearby area. Near what? Why? Why would seventeen combat-type helicopters be concentrated in one unlikely rural area far from the nearest air base, which would have to be either Luke Air Force Base or the partly decommissioned Williams Air Force Base in Phoenix, 130 miles away? With all the unusual activity around the south side of House Mountain that weekend, it would be a safe assumption that that was one of the areas, or the single area, upon which the military was focusing its attention.

To backtrack a bit, about ten days before Memorial Day weekend, radio station KFYI in Phoenix reported that Senators Dole and Mitchell were seen in Sedona and were allegedly engaged in a high-level, supersecret meeting of some sort. This clandestine meeting ties in nicely with the unusual events the weekend of May 29-30. Coincidentally with this, a retired man in Colorado who spends a great deal of his time following clandestine government activity called an associate of mine and said that he had just heard a rumor that the U.S. government was preparing to move some of its functions and operations to the Sedona area. Again, so many diverse and extraordinary occurrences happened in such a short time span that one has to assume a connection.

Furthermore, on Memorial Day weekend one of the largest hotels in Sedona was booked solid by FBI agents on short notice — so many agents that a person had to be assigned to locate lodgings for them in other area motels and hotels. What were Senators Dole and Mitchell, a raft of FBI agents and 17 attack helicopters doing in the Sedona area, in an out-of-the-way, rather average American town in the same time frame? Those activities alone suggest something of extreme significance, something the general public was not informed of, to be sure.

This next incident took place in Sycamore Canyon, a 33-mile-long canyon three miles northeast of Cottonwood. This incident happened on Memorial Day, the 30th. I'll call this man Ray. Ray is in his late twenties and is the son of a local rancher. Deciding to hike into Sycamore Canyon, he left the ranch at 7:30 in the morning. The going was a little slower than he had anticipated, so that he was only about halfway to his destination by late afternoon. The sun was low on the horizon when he noticed that high up in the cliffs something was following him. He said that whatever it was, it glowed white and was somewhat bell-shaped. It seemed to be trying not to be seen. Then things really got strange. He said that he soon came upon the carcass of a dead animal about the size of a young coyote. The carcass probably weighed about twenty pounds. What was odd about it, he said, was that it had not been dead long and looked like an animal that was half cat and half fox or coyote. Even more odd was the fact that its stomach seemed to have been removed by someone or something—there was only loose skin and a hollow cavity where the stomach had been.

As he continued down the canyon, high above and to the right two white-glowing, triangular-shaped craft appeared. They made no sound and seemed to float along the canyon rim high above him. Then, he said, it took him five or six hours to walk a distance of just over a mile. He doesn't remember, but he feels he may have had as much as five hours of missing time.

This is not the first time this sort of thing has happened there. Almost an identical incident involving two Cottonwood men took place ten years ago in the same general area. Ray did not know these men.

A week before May 30 a local couple had gone to an isolated location to inspect some property they were interested in purchasing. There were a number of buildings on the sale property, and as they were going through the buildings they discovered some papers on the floor of one of them, a small cottage. Most of the papers had handwriting on them and appeared to have been left by someone who had spent some time in the cottage. On one of the sheets of paper was written "Abduction is the Art of the Kidnapper." A connection to Ray's experience?

Two other Memorial Day weekend reports involved people being stopped at gunpoint by military personnel deep in the canyons west of Sedona. Before I go into those incidents I should explain the topography of the Sedona area to give the reader a better mental reference. To the south of Sedona is mostly open desert, with a few high, forested mountain ranges spaced here and there all the way to Mexico. To the north and east lies the Mogollon Rim, which is the southernmost edge of the Colorado Plateau—the largest plateau in the world. The Mogollon Rim is an almost vertical wall, created by earth movement in prehistory, and is punctuated here and there by a series of canyons. The Rim is at an elevation of 6000 feet, whereas Sedona's elevation is 4500 feet. To the west of Sedona are the famous canyonlands. These are Sterling Canyon, Bear Sign Canyon, Secret Canyon, Long Canyon, HS Canyon, Boynton Canyon, Fay Canyon, Red Canyon, Hartwell Canyon and Lincoln Canyon. Most of these canyons originate at Secret Mountain, which can be likened to the hub of a wagon wheel. The deeper canyons are like spokes radiating to the east, west and south. The Colorado Plateau connects to Secret Mountain from the north.

In one incident three people were riding mountain bikes on May 28 and suddenly encountered a number of military types dressed in black uniforms with no insignia, armed with M-16 military assault rifles. The bikers were about a mile from the mouth of Secret Canyon. They were told they were in an area they shouldn't be (this is in Coconino National Forest) and to turn around and go back the way they had come. They did. I have since learned that the U.S. military, at least elite units, do indeed wear black uniforms when guarding sensitive areas or installations. I have been told by an ex-army intelligence officer that elite army units do operate in the Secret Canyon area. Furthermore, I have been told by another military source that military personnel have to have a top-secret clearance to go into that area. Why? No one knows.

On the 29th or 30th I got a report that two off-duty policemen were hiking to the east of Secret Canyon in nearby Sterling Canyon and ran into a young, armed, U.S. Marine who reportedly told the two officers they could go no further. This is the tenth incident of this type I know of that has occurred in that same general area in the past five years. I have been told by a military source that a U.S. citizen (or anyone else) has a lawful right to demand, in a situation such as I just mentioned, the soldier's name, rank and specific orders as to why he is there. But, I suppose, with an M-16 pointed at your nose you're not likely to want to push it.

In yet another Memorial Day weekend incident, a Cottonwood woman gave me the following report in a taped interview. "At 9:35 p.m. May 30 my son (a design engineer) and I were out in the front yard star gazing at the sky. I was looking through my binoculars when all of a sudden a streak of light came from the direction of Sedona. It was soon over my driveway. When I saw the streak approaching, I thought it was a single light. But when I honed in on it through my binoculars, I saw that it was actually two vessels, one

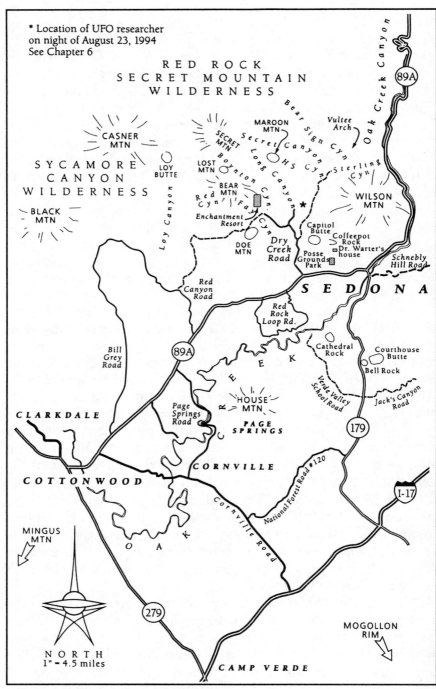

Figure 4. Map of Secret Canyon area.

right on the tail of the other. The one in the front was a ball of white light. It looked as if they were going to crash into each other. Then they started maneuvering. I thought the one in the rear was a jet plane. I could hear the engine on one but not the other. The one in back had two white running lights. I had expected to see red or green, which I thought was mandatory, but the lights were both white." (Author's note: Jet fighters can display just about any combination of running lights. They can be steady all-white, all-red, flashing red, green or white strobe lights or any combination of these or still other mixed combinations. I have often seen jet fighters flying at night at high speed with no running lights at all. I am not certain what the F.A.A. regulations are, but I would wager that fighter pilots ignore them at will.)

"From the tail end of the jet in the rear there was a continous red glow or flame, as though the pilot kept igniting the afterburners to keep up with the ball of white light. It appeared to be trying to ram the ball of white light. It actually looked like they were mad at each other. It looked like they were trying to kill each other up there. The white sphere of light was about the same size as the jet, maybe a little bigger, but not a lot." (Author's Note: Most jet fighters have a wingspan of about thirty feet.)

"Only when I got my binoculars on them could I see that I was looking at two crafts, they were that close. Every time the jet tried to ram the, what I'll call, starship, the starship would gently get out of the way. It was as if the starship was toying with the jet. They started doing some interesting maneuvering up there that I had never seen before, the one trying to follow the other, but not too successfully. The starship made a sharp U-turn and the jet had to make a long, looping turn to catch up. The starship headed in the direction of Sedona. The jet caught up with it and they both looked as one light again as they disappeared into the distance."

The next day, Tuesday the 31st, at 4:20 a.m. Cheryl K., a Sedona resident, was on her way to Phoenix. She was halfway to Cottonwood on Highway 89A (near where the UFO and jet fighter were last seen) when she came up behind a trailer rig making a right turn onto Red Canyon Road, also known locally as Two Trees Road. What was unusual about this rig was that the truck was towing a piggy-back trailer — two flatbed trailers instead of one. She evidently knows trucks, because she said that this one had additional struts under each flatbed in order to support an extremely heavy load. (By law, 60,000 pounds is the legal load limit for a trailer rig. This one could have carried twice that weight — 120,000 pounds or more. Evidently this one could do just that, as she remarked that the truck was also unusually large. Military tractor trailers are bigger and they can pull far more weight than a public or commercial rig.) The large rig turned off 89A and headed toward Red Canyon.

Just a few days after that, a man who lives in the Red Canyon area was returning home at 10:30 in the evening. On that narrow and unpaved desert road, he came up behind a piggy-back trailer rig. It looked brand new, he said, and it was pulling two flatbed trailers. On each flatbed was a bright yellow, tall, boxlike container. There was a pickup truck leading the rig, and both big and small trucks pulled over and stopped when the local man drove up behind them. The man said that the whole thing was very strange. It seemed as if the trucks did not want him following them or getting too good a look at what they were hauling or where they were going. As the man slowly drove around them, he said he got a pretty good look at the whole setup. He added that there was absolutely no reason for a rig like that to be out there. There was no construction or anything else anywhere near that area that could explain its presence. I checked with some of the residents who live in that area. They agreed that there was no logical reason why a truck like that would be out there.

The local man passed the truck with the yellow containers and the leading pickup truck. He drove slowly along the road ahead to see where they were going. From a distance he watched the two trucks turn left onto Red Canyon Road and head toward Highway 89A, the same road Cheryl K. saw the empty trailer rig turn off 89A onto Red Canyon Road. The obvious question is, what was in the two yellow boxes on the flatbed trailers and where did they pick up or drop off their load?

I am going to include at this point some later sightings that I believe are directly related to the Memorial weekend events. On June 12, 1994, in the Page Springs/Cornville area, a dozen or so residents watched for thirty minutes a silver cylindrical UFO moving back and forth over House Mountain as if it were looking for something. Also on June 12, a Cottonwood woman observed a silvery-gold cylindrical UFO fly over Mingus Mountain heading northeast in the direction of House Mountain. On June 2 a helicopter pilot flying over a remote forested region west of Prescott (50 miles southwest of Sedona) said that he flew over a large contingent of military troops in an area where he felt troops should not be.

In the early spring of 1994 on a half-dozen separate occasions, airliner-sized military cargo planes were seen flying at treetop level across the desert near Red Canyon — usually at two or three in the morning. This was in conjunction with dozens of black military helicopters doing the same thing over an eight- or nine-month period. One black military helicopter intimidated a remote home-owner to the point where the man, out of frustration, got his shotgun and was going to try to shoot it down. The last straw was when the helicopter hovered ten feet over his house. The helicopter left when the man pointed his shotgun at the pilot. Also during this eight- or nine-month period there was an eerie buzzing/vibrating sound whose source could not be determined, from below ground or from the air. I've heard this sound myself, and it is indeed strange. This tone, or sound, moves in a linear, east-west direction from Secret Canyon to Lincoln Canyon, a distance of about five miles. It has also been experienced far out into the flat desert near the canyons. It has at times been so intense as to shake buildings for hours at a time, to the point of completely distracting the residents of those areas. There is no natural phenomenon that can readily explain this sound.

A Cornville woman, on a Thursday morning in early July, expe-rienced a dramatic sighting on her way to work at 9:30 a.m. As she described the event, she was approaching the intersection of 89A and the Page Springs/Cornville road when she saw a low-flying aircraft — which, by her description, was a delta-winged fighter bomber with clusters of rockets under both wings. The jet fighter passed low and to the left of her car and began to make a slow, rolling upward turn. It was tilted at about a twenty-degree angle toward her — one wing up, one down. She said she had an unob-structed view of the plane and it was a clear, cloudless day. She described to me how the plane banked and started to gain altitude. As the plane moved up, something on the middle right side of the aircraft flashed, as if a large part of the craft was mirrorized and the sun had reflected off it. She said there was this bright flash and then the jet simply disappeared, vanished into thin air. She waited five minutes to see if the plane would come around again or be seen in the distance. She did not see it again. She emphasized to me that most of the top of the delta-winged fighter was in full view, not traveling downward away from her.

The last two items I am sure somehow tie in to everything else in this report. On May 19, a week before Memorial Day weekend, a local, long-time wilderness guide and I were going east in a four-wheel-drive vehicle on the Vultee Arch Road just past the trailhead into Secret Canyon. This was a bright, clear day and the time was 10:30 a.m. An animal walked out in front of the vehicle and stopped to look at us, about 50 feet away. It probably weighed between twenty and twenty-five pounds. The animal looked as if it were half cat and half canine. It had short front legs and longer hind legs, which gave it a cheetah-like appearance, and a long upward-curled, bottle-brushlike tail. The hair on the tail looked about two inches long, wiry and sparse. Its body was grayish brown, and over most of its face was an almost apelike cream-colored patch. The face was foxlike, with a long, thin snout, small nose and foxlike eyes. The ears were like that of a cat, small and pointed. We both got a very good look at this animal, and neither of us had ever seen an animal like it. My friend made the remark that as far as he knew, an animal like that did not exist anywhere on Earth. In appearance and size it was very similar to the one Ray had found dead in Sycamore Canyon 15 miles to the west of our sighting. I checked books on Southwest animals and the only one that came close was a coatimundi. It was not a coatimundi.

Another odd animal sighting took place on July 8 near Red Canyon itself. Two local residents were driving on Red Canyon Road when an animal walked out of desert brush into the headlights of their pickup truck. A very good depiction of this animal was drawn in pencil for me. The animal was taller than a hundred-pound dog that belonged to the driver of the pickup. It had very long, shaggy hair over all of its body and a long, horselike shaggy tail. It had catlike ears and a rounded, wide catlike face. Nothing like either of these two animals normally exists around here.

These following events, sightings and incidents occurred during the weeks after the main body of this story was written. This update was added on August 8, 1994.

On July 13, a Cornville man who lives a few miles south of House Mountain had this very unusual experience. Late that night, he said, "a golf ball-sized sphere of light came up to my bedroom window and seemed to be looking in at me." He told me that the little ball of light seemed either to have intelligence or was intelligently controlled. He added that the tiny sphere was so bright that it lit up everything in the immediate area. His girlfriend also witnessed this episode, but from a window in a different part of the house. After four or five seconds the ball of light drifted away from the house in a zig-zag manner and then over some horses in a corral. The sun-like little ball lit up the entire backyard as it went over the horses, but the horses paid no attention; either they couldn't see it or they were not afraid of it.

During a public book signing of my four books at the Loft

bookstore in Sedona on July 16, a man called from California to tell me about a most amazing sighting he had witnessed in Boynton Canyon recently. (He has a Ph.D. and is in the top management of one of this country's biggest defense contractors specializing in space and guided-missile technology.) He told me that he had seen a UFO slowly disappear into a high canyon wall in Boynton Canyon. As he was describing this incident to me, local resident Mason Rumney came in. He is the only other person I know of who has had a nearly identical experience. Coincidence? I passed the phone to Mason along with a brief explanation. The two men talked for over a half-hour about their similar dramatic sightings.

It seems that during the latter part of July, in the Jerome area (near Cottonwood) there were men and women working in pairs who were asking questions about UFO sightings and whether there were any group meetings in the area to discuss UFO activity. The conversation of these odd couples sounded as though they were reading from a script.

It now turns out that there were two witnesses to the vanishing of a delta-winged, triangular jet fighter-bomber. The second sighting was by a physician's wife near Sedona. It was early July, she said, that the triangular jet fighter vanished into thin air as she watched it. So there were two witnesses in different places and times who do not know each other but who each have experienced the same event.

In two other clearly related incidents, a woman and her two sons watched as two jet fighters and a UFO vanished into thin air. On the night of July 27, this local woman and her two sons were on a remote hill near Red Canyon that overlooks a vast area of desert and canyons. They had gone out to look for UFOs. They said that at 9:40 p.m. a white-glowing UFO appeared and flew slowly in the area of Red Canyon and Secret Mountain. The UFO would disappear for minutes at a time as it went behind towering rock formations and in and out of adjacent canyons. Then about 10 p.m., a fast jet fighter suddenly appeared from the northeast at the same time as a second fighter appeared from the west. The woman and her sons watched the UFO come out into the open and accelerate rapidly toward the southwest. The two converging jets caught up and stayed with the UFO for three or four seconds. Then the three craft disappeared. The three witnesses added that the roar of the fighters' engines also ceased at that instant, and they fully concur on the accuracy of the sequence of events.

To make matters really interesting, the same night at almost the same time, a former Vietnam helicopter pilot watched a jet fighter make what looked to be a strafing run on something on the desert floor near Cornville. These two incidents on the same evening occurred several minutes apart and were approximately eight linear miles from each other.

The witnesses of these two separate events do not know each other. The following excerpt is from a transcript of a taped phone interview I had with the ex-Vietnam pilot:

"The jets came from the north straight at me. They were so close together that the red running lights looked like one. They made a breaking turn to the east, and when they climbed higher I saw the two running lights. Then I knew that it was two jets. On the upward climb one of the jets turned off its lights. That's what they do when they start an attack; the wing man keeps his lights on while the lead plane turns its lights off and comes down. That way you can't tell which is doing what. After the attack is made, the plane making the run turns its lights back on. And that's exactly what happened. It looked like they were attacking a stationary object on the ground. I saw that and thought, this is all so bizarre —what the hell is going on here? They were going after something about a half-mile away from me. I could hear the engines but I didn't hear any cannon fire and I didn't see any rockets or tracers."

(Author's note: Tracers are flaming bullets, used to see the path of the bullets. This does not rule out that the jets shot at something. If the wind were blowing away from the witness, the plane's guns may not have been heard easily. Also, the jets may have been photographing something. Another possibility is that one or both of them may have been firing a particle-beam weapon. Military sources say that it is 99% certain that some U.S. and Russian jet fighters are now equipped with beam-type weapons instead of machine guns and rockets.)

On July 28, my close friends and associates, Claudia and Mark, interviewed a very nervous Cottonwood man who says he remembers being abducted by a UFO during the early part of July in Sycamore Canyon. He explained how he was taken into a UFO and was placed naked on an operating table. On the table next to him was a woman, also nude. She seemed to be under some sort of anesthesia. What alarmed him most was that he watched a "praying mantis-like machine" probe with a pointed device at many areas of her body. Then the machine moved toward him, and his memory failed him at that point.

On the evening of July 31, it was arranged for Ray (whose experience is related earlier in this chapter) to be hypnotized by a psychiatrist. Ray had an experience in Sycamore Canyon where he thought he had missing time. I was present with seven others at the session conducted by Carlos Warter, M.D., of Sedona. Dr. Warter is an expert in this particular field. We felt fortunate to have a competent professional doing the hypnosis session, as these types of matters must be handled by those who know what they are doing.

The session itself lasted for 45 minutes, and during this time the only people present in the room were Dr. Warter, Ray and a fellow who was recording the session with a tripod-mounted camcorder. While the session was in progress, the rest of us went outside to wait on Dr. Warter's wooden deck, which affords views of Soldiers Pass and an expansive area of sky. While the others were talking, I found a comfortable spot and lay down on the deck to watch a sky full of storm clouds. Moments later I experienced one of the most dramatic UFO sightings I have ever had.

Lying there with my head propped up on a rubber ball and absentmindedly listening to the others' discussion, my eyes focused on an object that looked like the landing lights of a small airplane — very common here, as the local airport was only about a mile away. Listening to the others, I watched this light, not seeing anything unusual about it. Then suddenly the light stretched out like one might pull on a ball of taffy, and this funnel-shaped light bent upward as I watched, in a 30- or 40-degree angle. There was a pause of about two seconds, then a point of white light streaked off into space at a fantastic speed. This light or craft was about the same size and brightness as a large earth satellite. I have no idea what its actual size was. It took a few moments for me to realize what I had just seen. None of the others could have seen it because I was the only one facing in that direction. Later I told Dr. Warter about it. He didn't seem to think it was such a big deal, and he told me about some of his and others' sightings from the same deck. My sighting was apparently somewhat puny beside some of the things others had seen from there.

The hypnosis session had been completed, so we all gathered inside to see what was on the videotape. The following are excerpts from it. You will notice that Ray's information largely agrees with the channeled information (which I have now read) to follow in a few pages.

Ray is at this point deep in hypnosis and Dr. Warter has begun to ask him questions:

Walk forward into that canyon [Sycamore] and describe out loud the sensa-

tions, feelings and perceptions that come into your mind.

I see . . . like a glass . . . in the air. I am walking, walking . . . (*stops*).

Look through this thing in the air.

I see, I see . . . a triangle. I'm walking, walking . . . in the canyon. But I'm not in the canyon.

Where are you?

(*Ray becomes distressed.*) I'm inside something!

Can you describe it? There is no need to be afraid. There is no need to be afraid now, since you are watching your own memories. Just walk into that form and describe what took place, knowing that you are safe. You are safe right here, right now.

(*Still nervous, now breathing heavily.*) I am walking through this glaze, this mirror . . . it's clear . . . and . . . I see my body below me and I see the canyon walls! I am rising . . . looking.

Where are you?

I'm above the walls of the canyon. I feel something pull me up!

What is pulling you up?

This light . . . light . . . bright light. Pulling.

Please continue. Where are you now?

I can't! I can't! (*He shows great fear.*)

Remove all imprints of negativity of this experience. Go to the event objectively now. Look. Move on. You are safe.

(*Ray is mumbling, breathing harder.*)

You are doing very well. Please describe it.

I saw something. I saw a white head! (*Ray is speaking low, as if he doesn't want to be heard.*)

A white head? Say that louder, please.

A white head! I saw a white, oval head! (*Ray is terrified now, panting and twitching as he speaks.*) There's more than one!

What happened?

A light. I just see this bright light! And now I see two colors in it, a white color and a darker color. There's this light! A light right there —above me! Right above me!

Where are the oval heads?

To . . . to my! . . . to my . . .! *(He is again terrified.)*

Yes. Identify them. You are safe now.

Gray. Gray bodies! Gray bodies! Yes . . . they . . . *(He stops.)*

Do they communicate?

Behind them is a light — a light. A white light. There is a yellow light in front of me.

Do you receive any communication from them? What do they want?

(Without hesitation.) They want something from me.

Can you identify precisely what happened?

No, it's blocked. They want . . . they are just looking at me.

Are you being touched?

No.

Move forward in the experience now to what happened sequentially after that. It's safe to look.

The eyes, no! *(He changes to a calm tone of voice.)* Feel peace. I feel fine now.

Were you probed?

I think so . . . yes.

Do you know the purpose of the probe?

For reproduction. There is something I have in my right knee. They are probing my right knee.

Are you in contact with them now? If you want to, do so.

(No response.)

Where in your body or your mind is your contact with them?

(Long pause.) It's right here. *(He points with his left hand.)* In my left temple.

The session continued for another half-hour. Ray said that there was a monitoring implant in his left temple. He remembers being on a sort of surgical table with a revolving white light off to his right. The aliens probed his knee with a device like a long needle. Ray said that there was no pain with the procedure. When asked what the aliens' intention on Earth was, he answered that they were "exploring without being known." They are curious about us. He said that there was an erosion problem with their planet and ours, and they are pressured in some way. They told him they are here to protect us and to guard against a mass hysteria of humanity. There is evidently some sort of a warlike conflict going on between certain alien groups. Also, "something was getting ready to break and we would be educated to outside life soon." The session basically ended at that point.

On July 29, a fire broke out on top of Secret Mountain. The U.S. Forest Service says that it was caused by lightning, but no one I've talked to can remember any lightning activity that day. The fire burned for five days before an attempt was made to put it out. On Tuesday, August 2, fire crews were mobilized to fight the fire. Half of these crews came from New Mexico, as evidently Arizona crews were tied up fighting other Arizona fires. When the fire first began, helicopters were seen above Secret Mountain playing searchlights around the fire — an odd fire-fighting technique, as fire-fighting helicopters and planes almost never fly at night because of the danger.

In the early stages of the fire, yellow smoke was occasionally seen billowing up from the mountain. Wood smoke is usually black, gray or white. There are no man-made structures on Secret Mountain except the remains of a cowboy-era log cabin on the northwest side of the mountain. Near the exact spot and time the fire started, a UFO was seen flying low over Secret Mountain. The fire, named the "Lost Fire" [the fire supposedly started on Lost Mountain but an eyewitness account puts it on Secret Mountain], burned for ten days. At one point after about seven days, the fire got out of control and jumped over onto the Colorado Plateau. It had burned over 1800 acres of pine and elm forest before it was stopped by rain late on August 8.

At the height of the blaze, from Sedona Secret Mountain looked like an erupting volcano. Flames could be seen at night from as far away as 50 miles. From the time the fire began on Secret Mountain (July 29), all UFO, jet fighter and military helicopter activity has ceased in the area. Today is August 8. There has not been one report of a jet fighter, military helicopter or UFO activity anywhere in this area — after two months of almost constant activity and sightings. This seems rather curious.

In many writings I have done over the past four years, I have been saying that something extraordinary must be centered or based on Secret Mountain, due to a multitude of reports of very strange military and paranormal activity in that area. One wonders if whatever might have been there in the past has now been destroyed.

Because of the many unusual and paranormal events/sightings that occurred during the general period around Memorial Day week-end, one can speculate that there is in this area something that both the U.S. government and extraterrestrials are extremely interested in. Could it be, for example, an underground base of some sort? Or perhaps an interdimensional base in the same physical location as Secret Mountain and/or House Mountain? Could it even be an interdimensional portal or a doorway to who-knows-what-or-where?

From the information I have accumulated I would have to conclude that during that general time period of May 28-30, 1994, a flying craft of extreme military sensitivity crashed, landed or was shot down in one of two locations. One location would be the south slope area of House Mountain. The second location would likely be in the zone between Red Canyon and Highway 89A — an area of ten square miles.

Global Shadow Government

Zoosh through Robert Shapiro
June 4, 1994

Did a UFO crash-land between Cottonwood and the Village of Oak Creek around Memorial Day weekend? Was the government out here? Were they going to cordon off Sedona?

This happened recently?

In the last week. Tom said that several people had called him. He saw a flatbed truck with a strange covering. Someone told him they had heard that Sedona might be cordoned off. There were government officials at Enchantment Resort. There was supposed to be a physical crash. It would have been last Saturday or Sunday.

I do not feel that the origin of this vehicle was extraterrestrial. The term UFO, I'd say, does not apply here.

It was one of ours? From Area 51?

I would say that it is more of a . . . it may have been disk-shaped, but I believe that it was something operated by your own military power, which could have accounted for the security precautions. I cannot say that I believe that this was an extraterrestrial vehicle.

So it was one of ours.

But that does not mean that it is not an event to take note of. You must remember that the entire Stealth fighter program is an elaborate cover — an expensive cover, but an elaborate cover for the true intent, which is building, maintaining and operating a fleet of flying disks. I don't want to call them UFOs because the term doesn't apply. Flying disks are placed in the sky, I can't say really by the United States government because we're really talking about a private group that is utilizing the United States as a base and technology obtained from the stars. From my experience here, I would say this is some international group, what has been referred to as the shadow government.

So how far can the craft go from here? They can get in the sky, they can go to Mars and the Moon, where can they go?

They can go to the Moon, which is their primary objective. They can be utilized for clandestine raids, which they are utilized for now. They were used in the Gulf War. There was some speculation that the Star Wars defense system, as it's called, was used in the Gulf War; and while it was tested, the primary weapon system that was used to wreak considerable havoc was several of these disks, which were invisible — though they used beam weapons, very nasty indeed, against Hussein.

It is really a struggle for power. I am sorry to say that the real motivation here is money, and that the government that you call your own is also sort of a — how can we say it? — a puppet. The battle over drugs and illegal things, drug wars and so on, the whole thing has been an attempt to shift the monopoly for illegal enterprise out of South America first, out of the Middle East second, and into what is called the Golden Triangle in the Orient. This has been the objective all along. And you will notice that with all the talk about South American drug lords and Turkish drug lords, you never hear a word about drug lords in the Orient.

Where in the Orient?

It is essentially . . . I am constrained to say, in an area — if this is China and this is Thailand and Burma and Vietnam — Thailand, Burma, places like that. Thailand.

The reason for the Vietnam War was control of the drug trade?

Absolutely. Yes. On the surface it had to do with mineral rights and oil and all of that business, and that was true. But underneath the surface it was about drugs.

So one of those disks crashed? I was told that helicopters with rocket launchers were seen. Tom saw a flatbed truck go up the canyon with some kind of strange tarp on it. This is all part of that?

Part of the workings of the shadow government.

Well, the disk crashing, there was a crashed physical vehicle. Where? How would you describe the actual place? If we went to look at it now is it all swept clean?

I do not recommend going there.

Was it in Secret Canyon?

There are devices in place that would cause a person to have nausea. I don't recommend going there.

Do they stick things in the ground like flares so that no one can get close?

It isn't an electronic thing, it's more electrical and it uses extra low frequency to generate a field that would cause you to feel sick.

Can you say where it was?

I will say that it is slightly beyond Secret Canyon. That is as close as I will get.

Toward Cottonwood?

Yes.

Was it coming or going from Secret Canyon, since there's a base there with levels that go way underground?

Going from.

And it just had a malfunction of the power system or something? It wasn't shot down, was it?

All right. I will tell you that it was shot down.

By whom?

Extraterrestrials.

From where?

There has been a falling out in recent years between those who provided the technology to the shadow government from extraterrestrial sources and the shadow government itself. So what we have here essentially is truly a Star War.

Well, we know that underground at Secret Canyon, along with the global shadow government and military personnel, there are various negative ETs – Orions, Pleiadians, Zetas, negative Sirians and others.

That's right. But what you have now is an entrenched group of people who will do anything to preserve their wealth. There is a lot of surface talk now; by surface talk I mean essentially talk that people are making, trying to point the fingers at this group controlling money or that group controlling money. But this is all a smoke screen, though some people do believe it. The real people who are controlling the money are not members of any race or religion or ethnic group or any of that business. This is strictly something that people have fought for and struggled for and are pursuing by any means necessary to get the money, to get control. You might have noticed lately that the issue of control is up, even at its most innocent level. Everybody is reacting as if they feel controlled.

Yes, yes.

And even overreacting. It's a back-and-forth reaction, not just for you, but for everybody. It's like they feel controlled, they're controlling. Back and forth. The issue of control is up now. And that is why there is this drug war going on both on interplanetary levels, to a degree, and on Earth. It is an odd thing that if every person taking illegal drugs were to stop taking them, and the people were to stop taking the drugs that are legal — coffee, ice cream, chocolate and liquor, to name a few, because they are all drugs, you understand — if everybody just suddenly stopped, that would essentially be the end of the war. But the people, especially in your country, have been conditioned for years and years through media, subliminal messages and everything, everywhere; tapes, even your electronic instruments are creating anxiety in you and also suspicion, and suspicion creates anxiety. So what is going on is that everybody is being conditioned to become dependent upon either a legal drug or an illegal drug so that every single person that is alive becomes essentially . . .

A potential client.

That's right. Well said. There is a society, a group, there are people who are mad at the shadow government on Earth. They are mad at them not so much because they're fighting for control of the drugs, but because the "shadow government," and I'm using this term in quotes, they're not really a governing body . . .

Well, they do control everything.

They control, but they don't govern.

Right. They're behind the government.

Okay. These people have not delivered on their end. They said, well, we will do this for you and we will do that for you if you give us this technology. So they've got the technology but it . . .

Oh, you're talking about some of the off-planet beings.

Yes, if the off-planet beings would give the shadow government certain technology; then the off-planet beings would get something.

What did they want? What could they possibly want?

They wanted an absolutely ironclad, permanent right to mine the Moon and Earth.

For?

The minerals that they want and need. Not much different from the minerals you use, nothing fancy.

What beings? These are different beings from the negative Sirians and those who have the treaties with the shadow government, who are at the underground bases?

Well, I'll go into that in a minute. But you see, with the experience now of your capacity to get to the Moon more easily, the people on Earth are thinking, well, we can mine the Moon ourselves. What do we need these guys for? We've got the technology. Let them take it away from us if they can — that kind of attitude, you understand — and why should we even share the Moon, much less let them operate there, says the shadow government's point of view.

This is fascinating. This is stuff I hadn't heard before. Continue.

So what we have here, then, are extraterrestrials I'd like to call pirates, in a way, because I'm not really talking about a group of people that are from someplace. Just about any place you might be from, if you conducted yourself that way, the people from some level — past, present or future — of that place would come and get you because there are laws governing noninterference with Earth. Not only noninterference in terms of corrupting the civilization, but noninterference in terms of coming here and being exposed to the civilization. So you're under quarantine, you understand? Someone would come and get these people. Why hasn't that taken place? Because these people do not carry the banner, as it were, or the flag of any specific culture. I would rather call them modern-day pirates.

So they're like renegades from various different systems that wound up here somehow?

Renegades. That's right.

Under somebody's banner. Somebody's got to be leading them.

They have leaders, not names you would recognize. Out of respect I will not mention their names; not because I love them so much, but I have to allow them.

Okay, but can you say where the leaders are from even though those planets won't acknowledge them as citizens?

Mostly from Orion, Sirius and probably the most notorious and the greatest number are from a planet that would be called . . . let me get this in your terminology . . . well, I'll spell it, you can try and pronounce it: X-P-O-T-A-Z.

What system is that in?

It's beyond your time. These people escaped from that planet. Well, not these people, but their ancestors did, and traveling through time, even time travel can take a while if you're a long way off. They are far off and the planet is no longer in existence. These descendants of Xpotaz are essentially without a country.

How many?

About eighty-five. But understand the implication here: On the one hand, of course, you don't like the shadow government. But on the other hand, you would say, well, the one thing the shadow government has in common with you and me (for the most part) is that they're Earth people. And the implication here, and it wasn't missed by the shadow government people, is that if these extraterrestrial pirates are given an absolute, unequivocal guarantee that they can mine the Moon and Earth at will, what's to prevent them from just taking over? That may very well have been part of the motivation of the extraterrestrials. So we have to say that even people functioning in a negative energy, such as these shadow government individuals, might actually be doing some good, even if it's unintentional.

Well, they are. They don't realize it, but they're getting the planet together, a computer superhighway and, you know, they're getting us ready for the Federation, right?

In a sense, yes, but you have to understand that they're also feeding you electronically, physically, food-wise, everything, the maximum amount of intake to densify you and keep you dense. However . . .

We're going to break through that.

That's right. Because there are forces on the other side they cannot stop. It is a struggle. Remember, I talked about this before. There would be a struggle and there would be the invisibles, as it were, who would begin to become exposed. The odd thing is, the people who are in the shadow government (and these are real people; you don't see them because you see their henchmen) look like anybody else, and they do not really live in such grandiose ways. After all, if you lived in grandiose ways, people would wonder where you got your money. So some of these people in the shadow government, people who have their fingers on the button, as it were, these people are really almost anonymous. If they didn't have an absolute means of intercommuncation among themselves, they would be hard-pressed to stay in touch with each other.

In a way, you understand, we talk about these people, and others talk about these people in a sort of paramilitary way, as if they were like military, because that's the way they're structured. Really, calling them the shadow government is a nice way to refer to them because in reality they are actually highly organized; taken beyond the level of organized crime, they are highly organized crime.

The ultimate organized crime.

Yes, the ultimate. And they are influential with many groups.

So then you could say that organized crime as we know it survives because it's tied to them, right? It's like it goes up levels to them?

Yes, it's a ladder. And not to paint too dark a picture, but many of your large professional organizations are seriously influenced by these people, too.

State what kind of organizations.

The American Medical Association is seriously controlled. They are trying to outlaw what is natural in favor of what is unnatural, and in the larger sense, they are trying to outlaw the practice of feminine medicine. Because you must remember something, and this is critical to understand the highly organized crime structure: *It is not totally, but is almost completely, male.* So we're talking about essentially back to the war between the masculine and the feminine here. It's an old war, and it's really well past its time.

Now there are other organizations that should be mentioned, too. The obvious governmental ones are there. I will say, interestingly enough, that even though they have attempted to make inroads with the motion-picture production people, and while they have managed to grab onto and influence some of the major studios, they have had virtually no effect on the smaller studios and on the arts in general, other than attempting to manipulate your various agencies, prices and costs and so on.

So some of the movies that we got, then, like Star Wars *and* E.T. *and* Close Encounters of the Third Kind, *were visions that were given to the men who made them and not leaked down by the shadow government?*

That's right. And equally, some of the movies you get (not the low-budget ones that people make on the side) that are primarily the grandiose ones with tremendous violence in them are supported. Not necessarily put out by, but supported by, the shadow government. Remember, their job, from their point of view, is to influence every citizen. If you can frighten the citizens sufficiently, and you can do that a lot with movies and television, and lull — that's the key word, lull — the people into believing that violence is happening more than it really is, then you can offer the wonderful solution to them . . .

Take away your guns, we'll take care of you.

That's right. We'll take care of you from the cradle to the grave; just give us all your power and be our slaves.

And those who watch those violent movies under the influence of drugs, that is total mind control, right?

Absolutely. Plus there are subliminal messages absolutely jammed into everything.

There still are?

There still are, yes. And television is really lethal. I know it is seductive and it is enjoyable, but it is lethal.

Why did they take Star Trek off?

That is simply a matter of greed. Not to be cruel, but it had been on long enough so that it was actually making more money in syndication than it paid them to produce new shows.

Okay, was anybody killed in this crash of the flying disk?

Two pilots. There was death.

How many on the crew of a craft like that?

Well, with automated systems, you can run it with two people, but you can run it more efficiently with five or six. A lot of these ships are still in the experimental stage and so just for safety's sake (and believe it or not, they do think about that; after all, you have to train all these people in absolute secrecy, so the pilots are a considerable investment. I'm speaking from their point of view. Those are not my values.) they were running what you'd call a skeleton crew. If you were going to operate all the navigational and weapons systems, you would want to have at least six people on board.

But at the moment there were only two. Was it shot down from underneath Secret Canyon or from another vehicle?

Above.

And what did they hope to gain by that?

Make a warning. Because, you understand, the pirate-type extraterrestrials, the ultimate weapon they have is force. However, the shadow government believes that they are bluffing, that they really do not have the weapon that they claim they have; plus, they believe that even if they do have it, they won't use it because it would be against their interests since it would destroy the areas they wish to mine as well as their threatened targets.

I thought at that time we were talking about the negative Sirians.

Yes.

They're involved in here, too?

Yes, because . . .

So the negative Sirians are all mixed up with the pirates?

Yes, but they're not representing Sirius. They are strictly renegades. Everything is all mixed together.

But aren't they all coexisting down underneath Secret Canyon on those six, seven levels down there? Don't they just live there?

I don't like to say coexisting. You know, just like in a neighborhood, anyplace, you might sort of coexist with your neighbors but not really be able to stand them.

I know, but when you're underground in the same facility . . . is it so big that they don't have to see each other?

That's right. They don't have to see each other. And, I might add, they've been expanding the facility recently. Some people have been feeling tremors under the ground but they've not been reported as earthquakes. That's why: because they weren't.

So they're expanding. How can they do it? Do they have a machine that melts the rock and then solidifies it on the wall? Is that how they can create new caverns underground?

Theoretically, but in reality, the people who are expanding it are really using Earth technology, so we're talking about explosions, which is why you get tremors. If you're using high tech, you wouldn't have the slightest idea. But they're not, they're using low tech.

Okay, so it's the United States, it's the Earth people that are expanding.

Yes, let's say Earth people so we make the United States government a little bit innocent here.

All right. So this thing is that big? I mean, we could see them in town? Obviously, the ETs can't come into town, but the Earth people could. We wouldn't even know the difference, right? We'd think they were tourists.

They do come into town.

They do? All the time?

They come into town when they need to get something or for R&R. It's almost like having a military base outside of town and the people come in.

But because we have so many tourists . . .

They don't come in a lot, but they do come in, certain people do.

Look at how well thought-out and how awesome that is. We have so many tourists. If it were a normal small town, they'd stand out.

Absolutely.

So they could be Eurasians, Germans, Africans, Indians — we're used to seeing every different type.

That's right.

What do the pirates do for R&R? They can't come into town. What do they do?

They don't come on the planet. They'd like to. Understand, I'm talking about a very small group of individuals here. They would like to essentially be the shadow government, but the shadow government is crystal clear about that.

That they're not going to be replaced.

That's right. And they're also crystal clear that the pirate ETs want to replace them.

Okay, so Star Wars technology under Reagan was developed against these pirates?

These and the negative beings from Sirius and any potential threat from space. As a secondary level, to justify its actual creation, it was to be used on Earth, but it was really meant to be used to defend Earth, so they had the ability to defend Earth from something negative, you understand.

It was their own private militia. It was their own private armament. It was

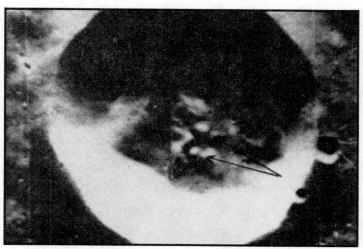

Figure 1. Two domes on the crater floor. NASA photo from Lunar Orbiter IV. No. 168-H3: "Lunar Backside."

to protect, it was to defend them.

Yes.

Right now there's mining going on at the Moon by these pirates?

Yes, and by many others, I might add. They are not alone. Mining on the Moon has become a really serious problem because I believe that this mining is having an effect on your weather. If you take enough matter out of this object, the Moon, which does affect tremendously your tides and your weather patterns, too, you're going to have a change in weather. So not only is the removal of this material from the Moon not good for the Moon as a being, as an entity, it is not good for the Earth. The shadow government would actually like to stop this plundering of the Moon.

So who else is plundering besides the pirates? Are they paying the shadow government? Are they coming in to take it?

No, the shadow government isn't making a dime.

They're just coming in to take it.

That's right. It's being mined as if it were open season, and it has been, really, since long before the human race was even present on Earth.

Why the Moon? What's so special about the Moon? Because nobody is living on it?

That's right. Nobody is living on it, nobody can say stop. And

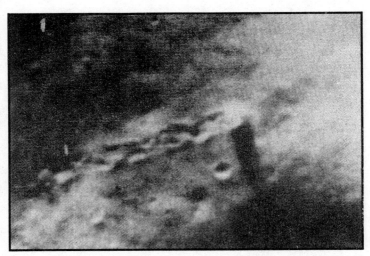

Figure 2.   NASA photo LO V. The large object leaving behind definite "stitch-marks" by some form of belted vehicle. No. 67-H-1135.

because it is made up essentially, not totally, but essentially of the same mineral substances as you have here on Earth, it's just easier and safer to mine the Moon. Of course, it's all going on on the dark side of the Moon.

So who's out there? What races? What planets?

There are several different ones. The actual mining is being done by people from Andromeda and from a place that roughly translates into Universalia. There is a direct project from — okay, here comes the odd name, translated again, it sounds like Scorpionicus. These are the primary contractors, for lack of a better term. They dig it out, but the material goes wherever it's needed.

So everyone comes to buy it, sort of like a store.

Yes. It's just like any other mining operation.

So there's a civilization there, then. There's a place where people live and maintain themselves . . .

Yes.

All underground?

Yes, but there is evidence on the surface. There is a book about the discovered bases on the Moon. Those pictures are real. [Note: *We Discovered Alien Bases on the Moon* by Fred Steckling, Adventures Unlimited Press, 1981.]

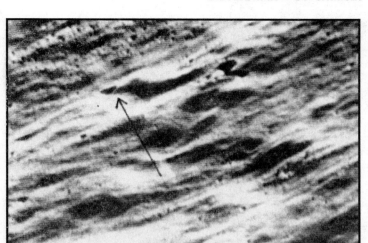

Figure 3. NASA Apollo photo 16-19273. Northeast of the King Crater. Notice dust blowing out of crater, upper left. "Who is mining the Moon?"

Those pictures are real?

Yes. Well, all he did was publish pictures taken by NASA. The pictures were, for the most part (not totally, but for the most part) at that time in the public domain. You go get them, you ask permission, you want to examine the pictures, the pictures are available at different universities, and you examine them and you find, you know, anomalies, meaning spheres. Spheres are not normally rock.

And NASA didn't realize this, or they just couldn't stop it?

Who didn't realize it?

NASA. When the book came out.

They didn't realize it. They weren't looking for it. Even though NASA is essentially a private company, it is supported by government contracts. It's a pseudo-governmental organization, so there's a limit to what they can keep secret. They can keep some things secret and they do, certainly. In order to work for the military, they must. And yet, a lot of those pictures were initially taken on the early missions, and at that time things were more innocent.

Is this the first time the pirates have shot down a shadow government craft?

No.

No?

No, this is perhaps the latest of five. That's part of the reason the

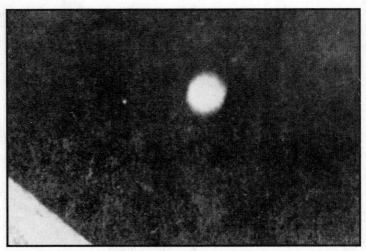

Figure 4.　　Apollo 13 photo of unknown glowing object near the Moon. NASA No. AS 13-60-8622.

base is being expanded — because the base is so active and because the Sedona area has traditionally been a place where there are underground extraterrestrial bases. It is a known place. You might say it is a known hangout for ETs. And it is also a highly sensitive place for Mother Earth. Mother Earth herself uses various of these rocky outcroppings to transmit energies to other planets, other beings. She is alive, you know.

She transmits knowledge to other planets? That's an awesome thing to say. To other beings?

Planets are alive. Everything is alive. The primary means of identifying a being of consciousness is simply that you can communicate with it, meaning that you can have a conversation. But a secondary level of a being of consciousness might be that you can say something and it will obey, meaning a pet or something like that, or potentially a child. Ask any parent. That's my little joke. Also, if you are from another planet, or you're a highly trained spiritual person, for instance, you would be able to communicate directly, telepathically, with what appears to be a rock, otherwise known as a portion of planet Earth. This, then, suggests that Mother Earth herself is alive, can communicate, radiates energies to other beings like herself, other planets, and has the total capacity to give you knowledge and wisdom herself if you choose to strike up a conversation.

So how does she feel about these beings digging down in there and warring underground?

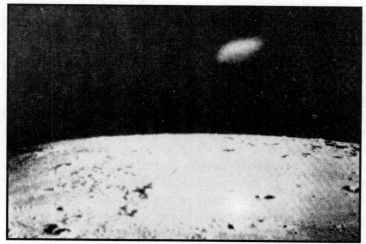

Figure 5.   Strange white aerial object high over the lunar surface.
As photographed by Apollo 12. NASA No. AS 12-51-7553.

She doesn't like it one bit. She doesn't like anybody digging in her, taking anything out of her at any time. She doesn't mind people drinking her water, because it comes back. You understand, that kind of thing is okay.

But this whole planet is tunneled. There are caverns and tunnels underground all over the entire planet, aren't there?

Yes, and it's not going to be something that she's going to put up with indefinitely.

Okay, so in what period of time have they shot down five planes? A day, a week, a month, a year?

They have shot down, over the past four and a half years, five of these flying disks. That's a lot when you don't have too many. That's probably more than 10% of their fleet. In military terms, if someone were to shoot down 10% of all of the military jets of the United States, it would be a disaster. So needless to say, the shadow government is taking the threat very seriously.

Supposedly, several very high-ranking politicians were at Enchantment over the weekend.

It is very easy to get high-ranking officials into Enchantment through the tunnel system. Enchantment, you understand, is sort of a front.

Enchantment is a front?

Yes. Regardless of who owns it.

Which is why the RTC took it over?

Well, it just makes it easier to have the government own it, even though it's a branch of the government that's a little bit independent. It's easier, but the reality is that even if you were to buy it and run it as a resort, as it has been, you're sort of buying something while somebody else has a right of use in the contract. So it's like yes, you can run it as a resort, but when these people want to use it for something, they're going to use it and that's that. You can't do anything about it as the owner. That's part of the reason, probably half the reason, why no one can really make that property work financially — because you're strapped by the clauses of the government saying we're going to use it when we want to use it.

So the people who owned it before knew? When you buy it you have to know about this, then?

Yes, you know about it, but it's presented to you in the most innocent and innocuous terms. You understand that no one would buy it if they were constantly threatened, so it's not like that. But let's just say that it's not an easy business to run and, to be perfectly honest, anybody who's ever done business and run this place ought to receive a check from the government by way of compensation, just to pay them for the losses they've had to suffer.

So you can get down underground from Enchantment?

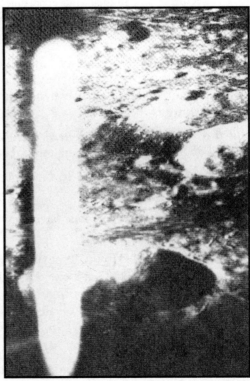

Figure 6. NASA Apollo 16 Hasselblad photo of cigar-shaped aerial object flying over the lunar surface. Picture No. 16-19238.

You don't actually get underground right from Enchantment.

Figure 7. Strange white, glowing, oval object hovering over Apollo 12 astronaut. NASA No. AS-12-497319.

They could, and they'd like to (you know there are some private homes still out there), but it's easier for them to just kind of show up. There are a lot of means, you know. You drive a vehicle out of something and who's to say where the vehicle came from?

You mean the entrance to Secret Canyon is so big you could take like a C-47 that had a car in it and fly it down there and then just drive the car? Is that what you're saying?

No, that's not necessary. You understand, the tunnel system leads quite some distance away. Let's just say this: You know where the Navajo Depot is? It is a military base not too far from Flagstaff. Right now it's being changed over to a National Guard base or something like that, but it is essentially a military base. You could land a plane there, discharge the people on the plane who might be dressed like anybody who would get off there, or land a helicopter there, and the people would get off and get into a vehicle and drive somewhere.

It wouldn't be difficult to disguise a means of their driving into one of these tunnels, and from that point on, other than driving underground, it'd be just like you're out for a drive. And you can drive essentially from that base or any of a number of various clandestine places where one might land a helicopter and access the tunnel system. You just drive along and you come to this place.

How do you get up to Enchantment, then?

You drive to Enchantment underground.

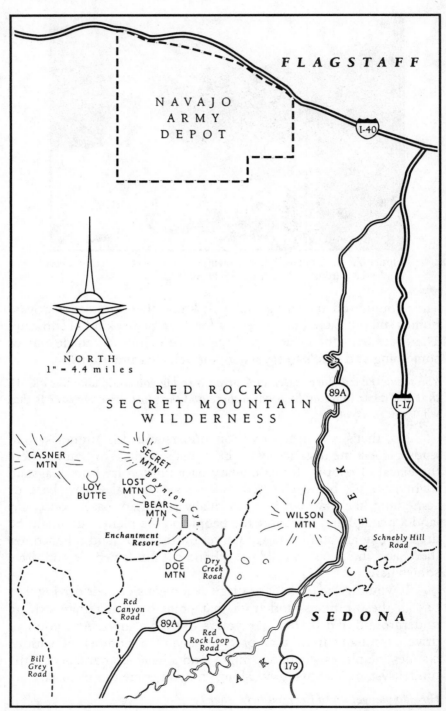

Figure 8.   Map of Sedona-Flagstaff area.

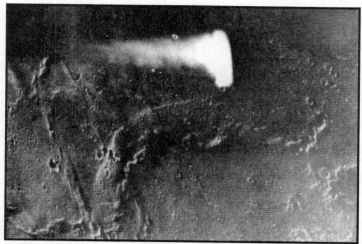

Figure 9.   Apollo 11 photo of glowing cigar-shaped object close to the moon. NASA No. 11-37-5438.

Then how do you get up on top? Say you want to go and have lunch.

The tunnel has access, you understand. Just think of it as a garage door, even though it's considerably more sophisticated.

For a long time now, the government has had the capacity, and other civilizations before you had the capacity, to have military bases inside mountains. The military naturally loves that kind of thing. It sounds very much like a giant conspiracy, but when you think about what is involved, and when you think about taking it back to its infinitesimal level —how often, for the best of reasons, do even friends deceive each other? A surprise birthday party is a deception, even though it is done benevolently. You must remember, and it is a tough thing to say but it is really true, that a certain amount of deception, even benevolent deception, is natural in the human race as you now exist. So if you take it to extreme levels, you know, it can get out of hand.

So you've got these pirates who are mostly based underground at Secret Canyon rather than at . . .

The pirates are not based underground.

Where are they?

They are not based underground at Secret Canyon. They are not based on Earth at all. The closest thing to a base that they have is on the Moon, because they're mining the Moon. The shadow government can't really do anything about it.

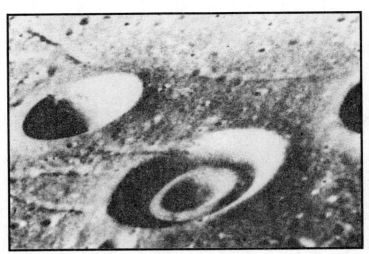

Figure 10. Apollo 15 photo No. 15-12640. The double-ringed crater in the larger Humboldt Crater. This one looks very artificial. Mining or more likely the product of high-yield explosion. (Atomic, perhaps?)

But there are all kinds of beings from Orion and other places underground in Secret Canyon.

But we are not talking about beings who owe their allegiance to a culture or star system or a planet.

All right. So the pirates gave the shadow government technology? I thought it all came from the ones they were allied with, the Orions and the Sirians and the ones who were underground.

No, it comes from different places. Consider this: Right now all the nations in the world that have nuclear bombs don't want North Korea to have nuclear bombs, and so they're trying to control another independent country, trying to control North Korea and say they can't have nuclear bombs.

Now put yourself in the position of the shadow government. If all the extraterrestrial forces you've been dealing with are trying to keep you from having the weapon system that you want, you might be inclined — especially if you had no moral principles whatsoever, other than a certain loyalty to having money and a certain necessary loyalty to each other — to get that weapon system anywhere you could. And that's where pirates come in. It's like, oh, we'll steal it, we'll get it for you, we'll even show you how to use it, almost — meaning that the weapon system the shadow government has now they don't know exactly how to use. And since it doesn't come with instructions and someone has to tell you how to use it, and since it is something that is somewhat activated by thought, then it's not only *what* you think, but *how* you think it that makes it work. And if it's something like that, then the pirates have not told them everything about how to use it. That's their ace in the hole.

Of course, the second level of that is that the pirates do have the capacity to essentially push a button in their ship (I'm calling it push a button, even though it's something else) and one of the flying disks of the shadow government just explodes.

And that's what happened out here?

That's right.

It wasn't shot down, it was push a button?

It was essentially push a button. There was no exchange of energy other than telepathic energy.

So the Earth disk pilots are going to get a little afraid to fly, aren't they?

You know they are. They're being paid a tremendous amount. Talk about hazardous pay, the hazard is extreme.

And the excitement of something new and secret that nobody else knows . . .

Oh, it's very exciting. It's beyond the leading edge.

Okay, so that's one level, but then on another level the beam weapons that they used in the Gulf War – the United States has learned how to use them?

Yes.

Okay, but are most of these at Area 51? Isn't that the training base?

Well, it used to be, but you know, everybody knows about it now, so it really isn't anymore. A place that is so openly known that everybody and his brother is out there with their video cameras — that's not very secret.

So it was?

It was the place.

Why can't you say where it is now?

The only thing I can say about it is this: It's hidden in plain sight and uses optical illusion to keep from being noticed. Understand that if you have an unlimited amount of money and can tap great and powerful minds (and that's very easy to do under the guise of government grants to universities, then people, innocent people, innocent scientists at the universities are working on some little piece of this project, having no idea of its real purpose), you can develop technology to its nth degree. It is essentially using the same system that the flying disks, not only from the shadow government but also from other planets, use to escape detection.

The Stealth.

Not the Stealth. No, the flying disk itself is able to be invisible.

Invisible through optical illusion. So it's way beyond the magnetic generators of the Stealth and the Philadelphia Experiment – way, way, way beyond it.

That was very unstable. This is something that can be done predictably, with stability, and it doesn't matter what the people inside are doing. So it's highly technological.

So you're saying that in the Gulf War these disk ships were totally invisible to anybody and they went around killing people and shooting up buildings?

Let's just say they were tested. You have to understand that it appears that Hussein was the target and they tried to kill him with conventional warfare, but just go down inside the Earth far enough, and there's not much they can do. The next best thing would be to eliminate him as an economic threat, and too bad for the people. It's like, "Don't worry, we'll just blow him away." You have to understand this kind of ruthlessness does not care at all about human suffering.

The thing to remember is this: Eventually these people – the shadow government, the pirate ETs, the underground coalition, everybody – will become gradually affected because Mother Earth does have the final word, and she will be pulsating regardless of all of the attempts to disrupt her. She will be pulsating and they will be transformed. People get used to their lifestyles; even if they know something isn't good for them, they will sometimes do it because they love it so much, even at the daily level. Regardless, Mother Earth will have the last word.

So the controlling group, the secret government, has to keep the shot-down disk and keep it secret not just from the citizens but also from the pirates and the other Earth and ET people who are part of the program. They don't want anybody to know about it.

They would just like to keep it as discreet as possible. You have to remember that the cover of saying that everybody who sees UFOs is crazy also works very well to keep publicity away from your most secret weapons.

I read a book a few years ago about a white woman in South Africa after World War II who met and had a child by a spaceman from Alpha Centauri.

He visited her several times, and often there was a flying disk with a Russian or German crew that tried to intercept her and the spaceman. I asked you once about this and you said it was a true event. So have we had that technology on this planet since the 1940s?

Don't forget that these vehicles can travel in time.

So one of the vehicles that she saw came back from our time? These vehicles can travel in time? The ones right now, like the one that just got shot down?

Scary, isn't it?

Fascinating. With no problem going or coming? They just do it?

No problem.

Are they flying back and forth right now in time?

Yes. They can do it if they perceive that there is some value in it for them. Pretty scary. That's why it has to be changed.

Yes, scary but also awesomely, adventurously exciting! Pilots right now that are piloting these things are doing that? Are they coming back and telling about it?

Yes.

What do they see as an important place in the past or future to go to?

Any place where money can be made.

Give me some examples.

For example, think about the great gold strikes in California. Suppose they were to fly back a thousand years before the gold was found, pick it all up and bring it back.

Have they been doing things like that?

They could. They're not doing it now, but they could do it. They're using these flying disks essentially for protection because they have a threat. But since they can travel in time, they can use them for any assassination they might want to do.

Have they done that?

They could. Let's just say they have not done so with anybody that you would remember.

But we wouldn't remember them if they killed or removed someone who could help us. If they did that — uncreated that — we wouldn't know it.

Quite right.

Have they done that?

I will say this only: The president who followed President Kennedy would have been someone else, not counting Lyndon Johnson, who was the vice president. There would have been another person in the guise of a Republican who would have been the president. Mr. Johnson would not have been reelected and we would have had world peace quite a bit sooner.

And he was eliminated before he was born?

Yes. However, that one act was, as they say, the straw that broke the camel's back, because now the shadow government is the object of scrutiny. Something is going on even as we speak, which is perhaps the most significant. That is that there are conferences going on right now that will last, in terms of Earth time, another few months or so that are determining whether the noninterference clause will be suspended to purify Earth of, as they would call it, evil forces. If this happens, there will be a serious struggle for power and there will be forces that seem to come and go almost in a dream, taking people elsewhere for purification.

These extraterrestrial forces of purification would come. I'm not going to reveal how. I don't want to ruin their plan, as it's valid; and they're not going to kill anyone, so I support it. They would come, take off someone who might be an assassin, for example, take him someplace else where he would be purified back to day one of his original birth. Assuming he had a normal Earth life, all of the influences that caused him to turn to this path of evil would be expurgated from him so that he would be essentially a benevolent, beautiful person. He would then be taken to an extraterrestrial society where he would live out the rest of his life. It would be a good life.

But with no memory.

No memory of that. I know it seems ruthless. What is to happen to his family and so on? If he is still attracted to having his family with him, then his family will go through the same process and will be allowed to join him. This will not be a heartless invasion. However, it will take place. People will disappear. If this takes place, it will be unprecedented, but there is a very good chance that it will take place.

At what level of conference are you talking about? Can you describe it? Is it like on Saturn or the Council of Nine or the Federation General Council?

I would simply say that it is occurring in the ninth dimension. That is the safest way to put it. I can't put a location on it.

Is what I know as the Council of Nine involved in it? Or is it way beyond that?

Way beyond. Including, but way beyond. It's more inclusive — councils that have to do with creation itself, angelic forces and all of these things. And that is why no one will be killed.

This thing with the Republican – is there anyplace where he was in the newspapers? His whole life was just . . .

Uncreated. So that's why you don't know about him.

Uncreated? When it's in newspapers and books and things?

Because those stories wouldn't have been written unless the person was alive, do you understand? They wouldn't have been written. You're not going to write a story about somebody who doesn't exist. So all of those things that were written never were. It not only uncreates the life, but it uncreates all that life touched, and a reporter writing a story would be touched by that person because he was writing that story.

Let's say this is a famous person at the time that Kennedy was assassinated. Everybody in the country would know his name. And I knew his name.

Yes.

But the stories were written. They were written because he lived and he was a candidate and a president.

Yes. And it was all uncreated. It is that simple. That's why it's so frightening, what can be done.

How could they take it out of the newspaper, and everything else in the newspaper would stay and that part wouldn't?

It's not quite so. It's not like there would be a blank spot where the story was. There would have been something else written there and the graphics would have been changed so you would never have seen it there. It's not just a blank space.

And this man would have brought world peace to the planet? He was that powerful?

He was influential, yes. You could not look into this man's eyes and feel anger or hatred. There was no way that anyone could resist signing a peace treaty that would be absolutely binding if this man had arranged it.

So this man was an avatar. This man was a great being. So they did something almost like uncreating Jesus, then.

Yes. You can't actually kill someone like this, but you can, using certain technologies, deflect that, meaning that his life took place someplace else. But his life as it would have occurred on Earth was uncreated. You can't kill the soul, but you can deflect it.

So he went to a probable reality.

That's a good way to look at it.

And that was just done twenty, thirty . . . well, why are they just getting around to doing something about it now if that was done thirty years ago?

You don't understand. The actual mission to go back and do this wasn't that long ago. It was two or three years ago. It was like, let's recreate it.

You're telling me that we had peace then? This planet was totally . . .

Yes, and even down to the level of the ordinary citizen. People were happy.

On this planet? Two or three years ago?

On this planet. It's hard to believe. And I can't convince you, I can only say that that's the way I see it: that you are living in a variation of reality that you weren't intended to live in.

This is why you were gone. You've been gone since 1991.

Let's just say it's why I was gone.

Say more.

When I said goodby, I was expecting you to go on to the next level with the leadership of that person who was at that time known only in certain circles. Then that variation of reality took place and instead of moving up to the next level, which would have created a benevolent past thirty years or so, you have this one.

I have the date. It was October or November of 1991.

Then I had to go with the other one. Essentially, I had to help him out. I knew he was coming to do all these things, so I can't tell you all, but we restructured his life so he can return. It will happen, and all will be as it was intended to be. But in a way, even though people are suffering now, it is for the better, because if you had made that jump to that higher level then, the shadow government still would have been with you and, more importantly, its evil side would not have been cleansed or purified. They have to have this last fling. They're going to get that, and then they will be purified. But they will not be killed.

Well you can't kill the soul, but the body will be . . .

You can only kill the body or purify it. They will not really brainwash them; they will restructure everything that ever happened to them in their lives that caused them to essentially be unhappy and seek fulfillment in self-destructive ways.

But the shadow government – they're still aware that they create bodies to reincarnate into. They've been doing this for eons.

Yes, when you think about their power, it seems very impressive. But in the larger scheme of things, their power is really not. It's very easy to eliminate them. Remember, I said you're living in a loop of time in the larger sense, millions of years in a loop of time, and you are dealing with evil. Let's call it what it is. So this is evil's last fling. It may be unpleasant, but if you look at it that way, it is, perhaps, a hope for some. And remember, you cannot destroy evil by killing it. You must purify it, and it must be done with love and benevolence. That's how we're doing it.

Wait a minute. I'm struggling to integrate the idea of this uncreated president.

It is like this: There are many ripples going on in your time line now because not only do you have the secret government interfering with your future and past and so on, you also have all of your individual souls interacting with your future selves, to say nothing of the influence of the Creator, the angelics and so on. So you've essentially got a whole lot of shakin' going on. This means that anything I say going out in print or even to an individual can create more of a shake.

Have you ever cooked something, a recipe, in which you had to add certain ingredients at certain times to make it right? It's like that. If you add the ingredients at the wrong time, things happen and the cake falls. So timing, as everyone knows, is everything.

But there is a reality that existed, even as you were speaking to us in 1991, in which there was peace? There was no Lyndon Johnson reelected and there was no – whatever the next war was – and . . .

Yes. Now it's a dotted line, but then it was intended to be your destiny. So you would have gone then, as it were, much more quickly to what you now know as the fourth dimension.

Let's back up again. What I remember is what happened. You're saying that he was a potential president?

No, no. He would have been president and he would have been

more than president.

Right after Kennedy?

Right after the end of Kennedy's natural term. President Johnson would have been sworn in because he was vice president, but he would not have been reelected.

So this man would have been a president. But would he have done all that awesome stuff to change the planet then, *or would it have been . . .*

Then.

Then. In the '60s.

That's right.

And that happened.

Yes, he would have won the Republican convention. You wouldn't have had President Nixon, though he may have served in the government.

But there's a reality that we lived where that happened? That I don't remember?

That's right. You must understand, if things are uncreated in time, you don't remember them. How many times have we said that you are living in a delicate, changeable time? Here's living proof: You don't remember. Now of course, it's just my word, but nevertheless, it is what I have seen.

I have read about that.

It, as they say, has happened in your lifetime.

And why has no one else ever talked about this?

Timing is everything.

Father To Call Back His Light/Life Force

Jehovah through Arthur Fanning
July 1, 1994

There seems to be circumstantial evidence that some sort of flying disk crashed over Memorial Day weekend. Is it good for the American people to learn about this? Is this something that you beings want out?

It won't matter.

It won't matter?

In this way: It is not a big news item, yet it is for some. Most of the consciousness of this planet is not ready for this information. It won't matter if it is put out. It is not required.

Well, will it do any good?

It will certainly do some good.

All right, can you give us all the details that you can?

What is going on is this ability to move through time.

Yes.

And these beings, these groups, beings, many . . .

What we call the secret government, right?

They are involved, and some of what is termed your extraterrestrials are involved also, know you? The Pleiadians and beings from Orion and others. And they are so involved in their game, having so much fun, you would say, in this density, the ability to move through time, that they are not concerned with what would be termed greater spiritual understandings. You understand? They are more concerned with *their* power. They're not into the concepts that you are — fear of death and so forth. They enjoy this manipulation of time, know you? Time travel, you say. This planet, Earth, being in third density, is one of the greatest playgrounds for these beings because you are enveloped in a system of time here, you see? So their greatest fun, their greatest game, is to play upon this planet because time is so rigid here; so they have a greater control of the rules, so to speak, here than they do other places.

Now, there is this great apprehension now that if the consciousness of the planet does evolve (and it will — it's going to shift to fourth dimension), then the playground of manipulation of time will not be available in the manner that it was. Do you understand? So there are beings that are attempting to . . . we will call it block the opening of the grid systems, to restrict the forces that are raising the vibration here to a fourth-level energy, and this is what is going on in these crashes. There have been several, not only one. And they be — you would term it battle, being how they slide on scale of time, so to speak. They may alter.

You are aware of what is termed seven levels of deities, seven levels of understanding, from this perspective, indeed? Your perspective, the seventh level is Father, you understand? Sixth-level deities (and there are only very few — three, four) are the ones that are involved in the focusing of energies to bring fourth density here. The fifth- and fourth-level beings are those that are playing in time, manipulating your time here. Some are upon the planet, most are not. Once you move into fourth- and fifth-level deity, entities, you have great power, and there becomes this difficulty to understand and an arrogance that you do not need the Father, and you don't want to pay attention to anyone, and you manipulate your game, so to speak.

In these times moving up now, these fourth- and fifth-level deities (we will call them entities, for they are gods here and part of the Father) are struggling in a manner fiercely to hold their playground, because when this planet shifts from third to fourth activity, there is this effect that others shift also. Now, those who do not have the ability to accommodate this shift, as upon this planet you would say they die, so too in fourth and fifth level of understanding. They transition not upward, but be termed to parallel universes. They are aware this is coming. They don't want it to happen.

It is not only that they are working with what is termed your secret government to truly control the planet, and there's going to be an outrageous financial collapse here at the culmination of this thing. As that happens, the game here will seem to be over. Yet what they are doing is they are creating a force that is going to create a great implosion inside the beings, inside systems, inside stars, even.

In answer to this question, there are these groups that are interfering with the proposed sequence of events, those things that have been determined from what you would call sixth-level entities to be needed for completion. Do you understand? They are interfering with sixth-level deities.

Now, the beings on seventh level are awesome power; they are there with Father. Beings in sixth level are outrageous power, and they have an arrogance, for they have the ability and understanding, the knowing to move unto Father; yet that is a place of no action, so to speak. The action truly be what is termed sixth level, great focus — ability to get things done, so to speak. You understand? Seventh-level beings must move through sixth, fifth, fourth, third to come here through their experiences, through their energy patterns, in a manner, to move back in time.

Those in fourth and fifth do not truly believe that the sixth-level deities are getting upset. They think that they've been talked out of these changes. It's not going to happen. From your perspective, you would say there was great disturbance, anger in the sixth level. From your perspective, not truly anger —annoyance. And there are these forces now that are working to truly call forth the Light out of these beings, therefore create the implosion.

Now, there are going to be more of these crashes, your shootdowns, destruction, and it is occurring not only in this country, it is occurring in other countries. Your Canada has had several already. Know you Canada? And your Mexico has had several already. It is last inning of game and great struggle to keep the game going, understand, here. So, how will I say you this thing? In this moving back in time, there is the ability to influence entities, and so they be not come forth in time, you understand? Yet these entities are well aware that those that have not been able to move forward in time because they have been . . . you play say die, these entities are well aware of the shiftings and parallels. They are not concerned.

What causes the concern is the manipulation of the consciousness of this system, with these beings, what you call the secret government trying to maintain the consciousness at what is termed a level of ignorance that is easily controlled. That is what's causing the concern out there. That is what is not going to be allowed completely, and they are understanding. You understand?

Yes. What they are shooting down is the global shadow government's flying disks which they have built with alien technology, right?

Well, what they're shooting down is each other. You have what is termed your trilateral thing, entities, and you have those beings that want, I will say, control in their own right, their own power. So they're creating a battle amongst themselves here.

Well, I didn't know the secret government has shot any of them down. Ah. Is this what in Zoosh's channeling we call the Renegades, the group that wants to mine on the Moon, or are there other groups that want control here?

There are three groups that are fighting for control, you would call it. One of them is upon your planet.

Those are the ones that are underground here?

Indeed.

At Secret Canyon?

They are indeed there and other places.

Okay. So there are the ones we've always known have the covert agreements, the negative Sirians and the Orions, as you've said, and the Pleiadians, and then there are these Renegades who want to mine on the Moon?

Well, they are mining several different places.

They are mining?

[He nods yes.]

Okay. And then there's what we call the shadow government.

[Again he nods yes.]

Okay, so they're all shooting. They're all at war with each other?

Indeed!

Even though the Earth people and the negative Sirians and Orions and Pleiadians are cohabiting here at Secret Canyon in the same big base underground, still they're shooting each other down?

They are into that thing, for they're thinking if they can create enough . . . they have what is termed agreement at times what is termed safe zones and at others everything is open to whomever. They each know, these groups, they must move very fast in order to prepare for these coming times. Now they are not interested in what is termed ascension here or becoming god or more god, do you understand? They already think they are, they have fulfilled self.

They just want to keep their playground.

Indeed, and they want to keep their sense of, from their understanding, what provides their force of ecstasy. For most it is control of other beings, and they slide on time. Time, in your system, is only available because the planet Earth is existing as third density. Do you understand? [I'll] make it a little clearer. Because the consciousness here on the planet Earth is third density, you allow, from a third-density perspective, third-density god, you allow your Moon and your Jupiter and your planets to be around you, do you understand? So your consciousness, as it creates from the god of you this planet Earth that you may walk upon and play, you create your stars. Now, when you evolve to fourth-level understanding, this will not be here. [He chuckles.]

The Moon and stars won't be here?

There will be an alteration, indeed, because the consciousness that is viewing them is viewing them at a different level.

Is viewing the fourth level of them?

Indeed! As you create that shift and what is called more of power from fourth, then these beings that are playing require third density to move time, do you understand, will not be allowed to what is termed, you say, live, because there's no third density here.

There will still be a third-density level after we leave?

Well, there will be a third density, indeed, but it won't be what you understand it to be.

I don't understand.

If they be playing in time — know you, back-forth time travel — they are still third density, indeed. You require third density in order to play time, to travel. When you shift to fourth, there is no time, know you? So you become the gods of they, indeed. So they be playing this thing to hold here, and what holds? It is your consciousness that holds and your belief systems and your fears and your guilts — not your freedoms. Do you understand? That's why we have told you many times before, it's important to know who you are. Desire to be more god, to be more and more, more. Do not concern self with other beings, what their game be, because when you do, you will never allow yourself to be more. You'll be caught into the game, figure out. It's all right.

So just as our third-density people who don't go into fourth have to recycle in third someplace, the fourth and fifth who don't want to move up will have to recycle into an alternate reality?

Into parallel times, parallel universes.

So it's like they can't graduate.

That be true. And they are fearful, for they have been in power for so long now that those of you on your planet who succeed to move to fourth, you are their gods now, and you're not going to be very cordial about some of the things they've done to you.

Let's talk about one of those things. Did they take a man who brought peace to this planet and discreate his life? The man who would have been president after Johnson?

We will put it in this manner: You may say that that be what happened from your perspective. There is no authority that can remove life. You beings play here kill a being . . .

No, no, not kill, but they discreated his life and put him someplace else, right?

I understand what you're saying, but you can't discreate the life. What they did, indeed, they put him someplace else, they shifted the consciousness here, you understand? This pattern that this being was to live upon this planet they took out, understand, so the time track that this one was to walk was not available. It was moved somewhere else and he understood what was going on. Does that answer?

Yes, but he would have brought peace? We would not be living in the times we are right this moment if that had not happened, right?

The times wouldn't have been as difficult, indeed.

The shadow government has more control, more power, more ability to keep us in density.

Indeed, they have.

Okay, so what are the guys in the sixth density who are getting a little irritated about this going to do about it?

Well, previously there was a squeezing of Light here to force it into entities, into their consciousnesses, to awaken. That has changed, for it was anticipated that more Light [would] create a greater vibration, beings become evolved. Now what is going on is that there has been a decision made, just recently, as a matter of fact, to call forth the Light that is within these beings home to the Father.

For mankind and any being on any planet is aware of this force that you call the Father, though they may not want to talk to it. Doesn't matter. But the force of the Father is what keeps all things alive, allows this thing, so the decision has been made to call forth the Light now and that is what I spoke of. There's going to be an implosion here.

Say more. I don't understand.

An implosion.

Yes, I understand the word, but how is that going to feel or how is it going to be?

Well, you won't want to feel it. It'll be an effect that those who have abused power will go crazy. They will know their Light be leaving and there is nothing they can do about it.

Oh, only in those who have been what we could call evil or cruel or manipulative?

What you term the intimidators and the controlling behavior beings. You understand? As this process takes place there will be great confusion, for it's going to hit many of what you call your political leaders, for they are involved, and there will seem to be anarchy. Yet it is God individualized realizing God. You understand? And as you go through this cleansing, then this peace thing becomes available and it also be where these ships, these rescuers will come, so to speak, and land and assist you beings.

Is there any time track that we can put that on, like the implosion will be when and the rescuers will be when?

Well, you've already started into this implosion effect. You're going to see a greater understanding of this thing in what you call your October of this year. In what you term your '97 the great ability once more to shift to love — choice — or not. In what is termed your '98, if the choice was not appropriate, it'll be a terrifying year for humanity.

Okay, let me just get some more details because there are people who will be interested in this. We can't find any pieces of it. You know, they come at night and take it away. There was an actual explosion of a flying disk between Cottonwood and Sedona over Memorial Day weekend, right?

What is your Memorial Day thing?

About four weeks ago.

I will put it this way: Indeed, there was this thing called a crash.

I will not say how it crashed.

Well, according to what Zoosh said, these Renegades who gave the shadow government the technology, have the ability from their craft . . .

Indeed, they do.

. . . to apply thought and literally disintegrate the Earth craft.

That is true. It is not the application of thought in that manner. It's the . . . if you'll recall, when we went through the black hole, how thought holds a thing; so it is a no-thought that creates the disintegration.

Oh! All right. I understand. But we've got people all over who have seen black helicopters and who have seen trucks carrying pieces and who heard this and who saw this, but nobody actually saw the thing crash. There's no witness to the actual event?

That is true.

And so this keeps it in conjecture. It's like nobody can actually prove it, like there are thirty circumstantial pieces of evidence, but there's no smoking gun.

Tell your man who does all this research — know you this one? What is his name?

Tom Dongo.

He be called Tom. Tell him to check in what is termed your Montreal area for notifications of what is termed meteor crash. Research that one.

Well, we were trying to get this one down, you know, sound.

Well, there are pieces available out there.

Is it around House Mountain?

It is.

Is it time for it to be known now that there is definitely an underground installation in Secret Canyon?

That would be all right.

Okay. And they moved the base for these Earthly flying disks from Area 51 because it got too well-known, but Zoosh wouldn't say to where. I have a feeling it's right in Secret Canyon. He said they use an optical illusion to keep you from seeing it. It's right out in the open, but the same technology that makes the craft invisible makes the base invisible, the same optical illusion. Is it here in Secret Canyon? Is it right here outside of Sedona?

Of course.

Of course. All right.

You've noticed there are a lot of new beings moving into what you term your Sedona. They're not all what you term third-level entities.

Say more.

Many are fourth and fifth. Many are from these groupings. They're trying to mix in, in a manner.

And how would we know?

One of your greatest abilities would be to be telepathic. You think a thing and watch how they react. It does not mean to create a battle here. You apply you, be body, you think a thing here — love" or you think a thing "Secret Canyon" or you think a thing "inside the mountain" and simply watch other beings as they look at you. They'll sort of identify themselves.

Aha! But they're just as dense-looking as we are, then, the fourth- and fifth-density beings? Not many of them look like us. Would these be Pleiadians?

Well, the Pleiadians look pretty much like you. They have the ability to shapeshift. Sirians are rather drastic-looking, however.

Yes! They have short ones and tall ones and all kinds. Where do they go for R&R? Do they have to stay on the base, the negative ones who don't look like us?

What you term R&R . . .

Rest and recreation.

They're coming to Sedona [laughter].

They can shapeshift, too? Even the funny-looking ones ("funny" from our perspective)?

Mmhmm.

They can?

Mmhmm. It is an ability of fourth- and fifth-level entities.

Oh, my god! So we're looking at what looks like a human but in his normal appearance he would be anything from a tall reptilian to a short negative Sirian, right?

Indeed. The only way you're going to catch them is in the ability to shapeshift. You must maintain a frequency and sometimes it is difficult to hold it all of the time. You allow your eyes to what you term go soft, know you, and you will see this when you look at beings.

All right. What do we need to ask that's intelligent? This doesn't relate to the flying disks so much, but there's all this talk of the U.N. bringing in the tanks — the blue tanks with the U.N. label — that they're unloading at Winslow. And there are supposed to be Russians in Prescott. Is the shadow . . .

Well, we've already told you that.

How close are we to a U.N. invasion?

Well, it won't be called an invasion, of course. As soon as this big quake begins to affect your California, that is when the government's going to step forward to . . . how will I say?

Declare military law or something?

It will be martial law because things are going to get rather crazy and it'll be needed to protect the citizenry.

So how soon is that quake in California?

Watch October . . . and watch May of next year.

So the drama is going to play itself out?

Indeed it is.

They're going to come into the houses and take the guns, and they're going to barricade us in the country, and all the stuff that we've heard about is going to play out, huh?

To a point, know you? And that point is when there is no more freedom and then it'll be called enough. It is important to play you here, know you? Understand your powers more and more. This is part of *your* game, also. Not that you fight, but you've come here, many of you, masters, to truly put your crowning glory on your being through the greatest density of all in this time.

So it'll be at the point when we finally get so tightly controlled and we say, "That's enough! I'm not going to take anymore!" It's like that?

Well, your Father will be saying it. Actually, there will be several beings saying it. [He laughs.] I'll be one of them.

You'll be one of them. Good. So what advice do you have for the people who read this, as all of this accelerates?

Learn to love God. Learn to love self. Learn to be free, not intimidated or controlled. Be free. Learn to move freely, softly, and be in love. Nothing will disturb you in that case. It might seem to, but it can't harm you. It may what you term hurt the physical body, and the physical body might become painful, but the purity of your being can never be damaged, and that is a truth. That is the Light that you are that is becoming more conscious here now. Many of you are beginning to communicate, whether you know it or not, from the Light of your being, and you're still throwing off some of the old patterns. That is all right. It's needed here. It is truly an empowering thing.

Well, Don Juan said, "If you want to grow, get a tyrant." So we have some good tyrants, right?

You've created some outrageous tyrants.

Okay, what else do we need? Zoosh said that they were going to take them off one by one and purify them.

[He laughs.] I like that word.

You say they're going to call the Light out of them. Is there a similarity there?

Well, you can figure it out. It is the same thing, understand?

All right. He said, basically, that the meeting that was going on was to see if for the first time the prime directive of noninterference could be set aside because they had gone over the limit of . . .

That is true.

That's the meeting that you said just ended, and that was the decision, to call the Light back?

[He nods.]

Okay.

Won't be a pretty sight. Won't matter.

But those beings then eventually will go through another cycle and will come back to the Light somehow?

Well, it's a little more confusing than that. What has happened is that they've already come back in time because they know they've what is termed screwed it up here at this point. Do you understand? They still haven't learned.

We're only talking about the negative ones now? What are we talking about?

Well, all of you.

All of us! We came back in time to fix it?

And the negative ones here, everyone. Because this is where the game is now. In this manner, some are getting it — desire for freedom, peace — and some still won't, even though this is the most fertile area to get it in, in this time, this planet here, your planet. The negative ones want to feel density even further. They don't want to feel it for themselves so much; they want to feel it so they can watch others in their agony, so to speak. That's not going to be allowed completely. Do you understand?

Yes.

Anything else?

All right, is there anything more that pertains to this? Should we print that information about how you can get underground to Enchantment Resort in Boynton Canyon? Is it something that the people should know or is it just gossip that the government figures fly into any base around here and then there are tunnels underground so they can drive up out of a garage and they're at Enchantment? Boynton Canyon is not their real destination, is it? It's because they want to deal with the people at Secret Canyon, right?

That is true.

Can you get from Secret Canyon to Enchantment, also?

Of course. This is not the only place this activity is occurring. It's also occurring in your Colorado and your Colorado is going to have a great bang here shortly.

Where in Colorado?

What you term in your Denver area, outside.

Outside. Is Dulce still active or is that shut down in New Mexico?

Mm, it is still active.

It is. Okay. And there are more bases besides that?

Of course.

Can you say more?

I could, but it would not serve anyone at this time.

Okay, but evidently it's time for the people to know. I was trying to find out if a UFO had crashed and Zoosh was talking to me about this president, so evidently this is information that people at least can focus on to . . . to what?

It will help them to understand that they are not as free as they thought they were, and it will also force them into becoming more of their own being. Some will get caught up in it — doesn't matter, you understand. But it is always wise to know a little bit more than you did before. And what is termed Zoosh has his energies to get this out.

Okay. That's good. Thank you.

The Shadow Government
and Its Alien Allies

Zoosh through Robert Shapiro
July 23, 1994

Greetings. What do you wish to know about the underground bases?

How many of the bases are there in the United States, and are there any in other countries? I'm referring to the shadow government's alliance with negative ETs.

I'm going to broaden that a bit and say the shadow government's alliance with others. There are really not that many. There are no more than five active bases and three inactive. When you have the equipment you need, you really don't have to spread out too far. You must recognize that the trend now in all the powers that be, including the regular government, is to build all bases underground. That's why all this talk in recent years about closing army bases and so on is not exactly real. Surface bases will be closed, yes, but underground bases will continue to flourish.

There is a shadow government base being expanded in the nearby region, roughly between Sycamore Canyon and Secret Canyon.

There's one situated within about 300 miles of the North Pole. That's about as close as they can get and still have their equipment function. And then there is one located under the sea about 450 miles north of the South Pole. They attempted to build one in

Australia, but their efforts were thwarted by ancient wisdom applied by Aboriginal elders who knew what was being done. Through magical arts that they alone on this planet apply and possess, they were able, in an undetected and discreet manner, without injuring anyone, to prevent that base from being built or occupied.

The one in Dulce, New Mexico, has been greatly reduced or compacted. This is largely because of the bases now functioning near the North and South Poles. Energy is gathered from those polar regions to power their equipment; thus, they are even less detectable since they are not using atomic power. They are simply using magnetic energy.

There is one in Iceland that is inactive at the moment. The one near Denver has been shut down, no longer occupied. They left a contingent in the mountains surrounding Colorado Springs, but it's very small, so the people in Colorado Springs ought not to be alarmed.

Now there are two other bases that are active, functioning. One of them is on a peninsula of Siberia. I will be more specific: It is not that far from the Aleutian Islands off Alaska, but it's associated with the Siberian continent. And there is one fairly deep, probably the deepest one inside the Earth, below the Cape of Good Hope, an area known for some time as a stormy place to sail. Those who would navigate the sea there did not particularly enjoy the experience.

I might add that the underground base is not causing that difficulty. It is a natural anomaly of Earth herself. But the underground base does derive a certain amount of energy from Mother Earth that they could use for a particular weapon they have. The energy in Mother Earth there is an energy that disarranges things. It is not exactly disintegrative, but anything that would flow in a natural rhythm is exposed to a window there, not only of its equal and opposite but also of its parallel; so it's essentially a disrupting energy. The people in that particular base have been able to utilize some of it.

Through use of a parabolic sound generator (which I'm calling parabolic so you can understand the way the sound wave is directed; it is not an actual parabolic antenna, but there is a parabolic wave) they can use this disrupting energy. They can focus it through a parabolic sound wave into fairly small and concise beams of about an inch, maybe three-quarters of an inch, that can be directed outward and will travel a distance equal to about 300 or 400 miles.

Beam Weapon Can Attack Flying Disks

This is the weapon that is the most effective for shooting down various flying disks from other places. It can also be used, for that matter, to shoot down conventional aircraft or even knock down a bird, if a person is feeling particularly malevolent and just wants to be cruel. They test the weapon on birds, I'm sorry to say; military forces have for many years tested some of their weapons on animals, as if animals did not count.

So this disruption sound beam —it's not actually a sound, but it's encapsulated in sound, which is the only way they found to be able to control it —is a serious weapon. You will have to ask more if you want to know more.

All right. If it can go only 300 miles, why do they have it there in such an awkward place?

Because that's where the energy is. They can't transport the energy. They can't create the energy on their own. The energy is naturally occurring at the Cape of Good Hope because it's an energy that Mother Earth herself has. She uses it to recreate her surface. If she needed to go utterly dormant for a while, the forces she would broadcast that say to sleep for several million years —which would destroy almost all life on her surface —would begin there.

Now, they can't tap it all. Right now, even at the maximum use of the weapon, they can tap only about one millionth of one percent, though they may be able to do more at some point. But even if they can do more, they still can't broadcast it farther than 300 to 400 miles, so there's not much motivation to do more.

Okay, let's get some statistics. There are five active bases plus three inactive bases. How many Earth personnel and how many ET personnel are in each of these bases?

Not that many ET personnel. You can understand that the shadow government would rather not have any ET personnel, so it's what one could refer to as an unholy alliance from the perspectives of both sides, to say nothing of an outsider's point of view. So probably all in all, counting all of the bases that are active and the bases and outposts that are being shut down or at least greatly reduced, there are no more than, in terms of ETs right now, perhaps 14,000. That's not too many, really. In terms of Earth personnel, of surface-born Earth beings, there are in the neighborhood of 80,000 to 100,000.

But there is a third category. In terms of genetically created subterranean beings who practically never come to the surface, there are at least 150,000. They would, for all intents and purposes, be perceived as slaves, for they do not understand surface life or the life of the heart, as they are not allowed to develop that way. So they would be what the military has always desired as a perfect soldier, solely on the basis of their skills. Yet if the militaries on the surface had these people, they would not like them because they have no heart. They would not commit an act of bravery selflessly. They might be wonderful soldiers, but they are individuals always and only. Teamwork is a struggle for them because they have never been allowed to develop bonds of friendship or love.

These are clones.

I'd rather not call them clones because they are not all the same. They look different

But they were made genetically in a test tube rather than being born from a womb?

Well, that's an oversimplification. They were not created in a test tube. They may be initially separated, sperm and eggs and so on, in a test tube, but the matrix in which they are grown is not a test tube at all. It is a solar-amplified chamber in which they grow, meaning amplified by an artificial sun, and they are crystal-balanced, meaning in this case attuned through the use of artificially created crystals. That's part of the reason they don't have much of a heart development. The crystals are artificial, so they're tuned specifically for certain skills rather than for natural heart occupations.

The artificial chamber is considerably bigger than a woman's body. The person grows in the chamber in a liquid. The liquid is not exactly water. If I were to have to compare it to a fluid that is known on the surface of the Earth, it would be just a little heavier elementally, referring to the periodic table here, than heavy water.

Within this pseudo-waterlike matrix grow these male beings — no female beings, not one. There's a reason for that. It's not just preference. The reason is that no female being anywhere, anywhere in all the universe, can be programmed solely and completely without love. Male beings can have this for a time, though they will constantly be searching for the missing part of themselves. If they are sufficiently disciplined, they will not spend much time doing that.

So that is how they are grown. Unlike a normal birth when you have delivery of a child, these beings are grown under high-speed techniques so it doesn't take years and years. They are grown and essentially hatched, as it were, or are brought out of the chamber at a surface maturity, meaning the surface of the planet. If you were to look at a being, you would say he is about twenty years old. This way they avoid having to deal with the complications of childhood, although it takes a good six months to get them through learning how to go to the bathroom for themselves and learning how to eat and so on.

Created Beings Are "Born" with Active Aggressive Hormones

In this way they are born into their aggressive hormonal activity. A young man has his hormones switched on when he is about twelve and for the next three or four years goes through lots of different experiences, some of them good, some not so good. And then he spends the next few years trying to sort that all out. Well, they "birth" them at about the age of twenty. They have discovered that this minimizes what they would call the adolescent experience. They are also born, then, with their hormones fully functioning and are essentially already aggressive. So they do not have to, at least chemically, be trained that way.

Also, certain hormones are stimulated. For their first five years of life, they are given testosterone in a homeopathic remedy. It is interesting to note that the secret government does use alternative medicine here! They do not give them actual chemical testosterone because that would tend to deplete their own. It would tend to negate the effects of their own organs, you understand. But a homeopathic stimulant to the male hormone supports and encourages more of this hormone than is really needed for a person of that age unless that person is designed to be a professional solider, in which case he becomes slightly more aggressive, which is believed to be of benefit to the secret government.

What good is aggression underground in a base? They don't come out on the surface.

They are trained to be enforcers. Let us remember that these people are not really trained to be warriors as you know them, because the chances of ever having a major war underground are considerably diminished compared to the surface. No, they are actually trained to be policemen, as it were. And they are trained to be fairly ruthless policemen. It would be something like a military policeman, all right? But without the understanding, without the compassion and without the day-to-day human experience that military policemen on the surface of the planet must possess. So they would be somewhat, perhaps considerably, intolerant of the ways and means of experiencing human life. They would look, for all intents and purposes, like human beings. And essentially they are.

They have souls?

Well . . .

Or the souls have them.

I would rather say that they have a diminished soul, for that is an influence down there as well. And they have what is called a stranded, diminished spirit.

Why would a spirit or soul occupy a body like that?

All life has some soul and some spirit, but the people who are generating these beings wish to have the minimum amount of soul ensoul them, don't you understand, and the minimum amount of spirit. That's part of the reason they use the crystal matrix and all of this business — so as to deflect the natural spirit that would enter the body. At the base of the skull and at the very bottom of the spine, the coccyx, are installed crystal devices, all right, which tend to deflect the entrance of spirit-soul energy. Nevertheless, some gets in; but not much.

But I thought the soul created its own body. Why on Earth would it choose to have this experience?

You have to remember these beings are created, how can we say . . . I know what you are saying — that all souls will choose, that before the form exists there is soul. But to put not too fine a point on it, before the soul exists, there is spirit. Then there is soul as form is taking place.

But these people are denied their natural growth cycle until they get to be twenty years old, and spirit and soul are greatly deflected. So the spirit may be present elsewhere and is constantly attempting to get inside the body, but is constantly being deflected. And the soul does not have a chance to grow through the interaction with normal human experience or life experience.

So here we have a situation in which the soul does not choose this experience. The spirit does not choose this experience. The spirit intends to have an upliftment of this being, but it's an uphill battle. It can be done, but it will take time and, essentially, it will take, at some point, interference from outside forces to ensoul and enspirit these beings fully.

So what will happen now in the next few years when we go into the other dimension? How will they handle that?

When that happens, those who have kept them in this form, those who are their creators, in a sense, will not be present. And while the bases are largely automated, for security reasons the machines must essentially be reset about once a year to continue to function. This is a proper security precaution. If the machines are not reset they do not reset themselves to run in perpetuity. Otherwise, there is perceived, by those who created these machines, and rightly so, to be a hazard because the machines could then essentially take over. Now, if after a year they are not reset by people, they will simply gradually power down and over the period of two or three years they will power down to the point where they completely shut off. They will no longer be sending the rays of energy that go to the implants in these beings and deflect soul and spirit; hence, soul and spirit will be able to enter. When this occurs, these beings will have a driving force to get up and go out onto the surface.

Now, there is a way to get to the surface. It's not easy, but they can find out, and they will eventually. It will probably take them a few months. They have plenty to sustain them down there so they will not suffer. They will eventually get to the surface. On their way to the surface they will begin to change. They will begin to fight amongst themselves, which they don't usually do. They will need to have teamwork and cooperation to achieve their trip to the surface, and this they are not used to doing. So they will essentially have to learn teamwork and cooperation from scratch on their way to the surface. And when they do achieve the surface, while they can then sustain individuality, many of them will want to continue with teamwork in order to create some level of camaraderie, which, by that time, they will desire, since the soul and spirit are always seeking others.

How deep are these bases? How deep is the one at the Cape of Good Hope? The living quarters are how deep beneath the surface?

About 150 miles.

So the military or the ETs come to the surface and then they fly down, they take an elevator, they drive through a tunnel? How do they get down to the bottom?

They don't actually enter from the surface. They can if they absolutely have to, but only through light devices, light conveyances, meaning the extraterrestrials can come and go that way. Also, there

are entrances under the sea. So we're talking about essentially seagoing vessels, submarines. They can enter that way. But, of course, the
simplest way to enter is underground through tunnels. That is the
means by which it is done. And I might add that because the bases
are so complex and so secret, in order to get to the proper tunnel,
you essentially have to go through what amounts to a maze. They've
built about 400 more tunnels than are necessary. There's only one
tunnel that goes there, but it goes this way, that way, up, down, back
forth. It's very much designed to be a maze.

We're talking particularly about the Cape of Good Hope?

Yes. It's to keep out those who are not supposed to be there,
from the occupants' point of view. The mazes, I might add, are not
lethal. If you get turned around and can't find your way, there are
not, you know, lions waiting for you. You just can't find it.

The U.S. military that comes and goes has to use submarines?

Yes. And I'm loathe to say U.S. military. I'd really rather not say
that. Let's say surface Earth people.

*Surface Earth people. Then the military complement has military from all
countries?*

Not really. This is a private, secret army. The submarine is a
private, secret submarine. It is not carrying the flag of nor is it
performing any duties of any military power on Earth. So it's essentially a private arrangement.

You know, it's an interesting thing, because if you ask any pilot
of a seagoing vessel or, for that matter, of a plane if he has seen
UFOs, oh yes, they have all seen them. Sometimes the UFOs they see
are actually vessels from this private organization, especially in the
case of these submarines, because they have full, for lack of a better
term, masking capabilities. You might see a submarine. You're looking at it, all of the lookouts see it, all of the radar sees it and the sonar
is detecting it. While everybody is observing it and the ship is going
to general quarters because they don't know who it is, it disappears.
But it's the way it disappears; it doesn't just vanish, it seems to shrink
and become almost a toy version of itself. It shrinks in space and
then it disappears.

And that's their optical illusion technology.

Yes, it's very much like a mirroring effect, like a hall of mirrors.
This alone tends to baffle a lot of the surface seagoing navies, thereby
we have essentially a UFO report, even though this is actually a

vehicle that I wouldn't call a UFO.

So where are the secret military headquarters for the undersea vessels? They have to build them and maintain them and repair them someplace.

Generally, they just steam in to the bases. "Steam" is the term I'm euphemistically using. Once they get in, then they can be repaired. You have to remember we're not talking about little bitty places. You know, in terms of area, the base at the Cape of Good Hope is about 250 square miles less than the size of the entire state of Rhode Island. So the base is huge.

What do they do there besides focus that disrupting thing?

And run the world?

Is that the headquarters? Is the Cape of Good Hope the planetary headquarters?

Yes. Also, it's an underground city. The ETs have their own colonies where they live and thrive in the lifestyles they desire. The Earth human beings have their colonies. And even those that have been created as "underground MPs," as we're calling them in quotes, they have their areas, too.

So do the Earth military have their families there or are they assigned tours of duty where there are just men?

Earth people, surface Earth people, surface forces do not have their families there. That would be a serious security compromise.

So they're assigned tours of duty there and then their memories are wiped?

They have about a three-month tour of duty there and then their memories are not wiped, but masked. This can be done with minimal disruption of the rest of their memory circuits, but they would probably have, for the next six to twelve months, memory lapses. They might forget when their anniversaries are or they might forget when their children's birthdays are. Their wives, for instance, or their relatives might remind them, and they would say, oh, how could I have forgotten?

Because the masking got a little into that area.

Yes, unintentionally. But it does. I might add that this is essentially the same process by which people who are UFO contactees do not remember their experiences.

Because the ETs do that selective wiping?

Yes, it's essentially the same instrument. Not quite, but at its core it's the same.

It's a technical instrument? It's not by thought?

No, no. It's a device.

And the secret government got it from the ETs?

Yes.

Okay, but how could you build that kind of thing under the Cape of Good Hope with nobody seeing it?

It's all done . . .

It's all done through the tunnels.

Yes, it's done either through the tunnels or undersea. You bring in some of your supplies undersea on these ships. We're calling them submarines, but we're not talking about the little bitty submarines that they had in World War II, we're talking about ships that are about two and one-half times the size of a conventional nuclear-pow-ered submarine in the military forces today. If you have seen these submarines, you know they are quite humongous.

How many of those do they have?

Really only about four, five. I'm saying four or five because one of them is always being repaired. Four out there and about.

Submarines have to go to someplace, so do they surreptitiously supply the ship? How do they supply the ship and the bases?

It's all done underground through tunnels. There are under-ground, undersea openings.

Do these subs come to the United States or to Europe to get supplies?

They don't usually come to the U.S. or Europe.

Where do they go?

They usually go places where there are fewer surveillance de-vices just so they don't have to deal with the UFO phenomenon, as it were. In the case of undersea submerged objects — I guess we should say USO — they generally go to more remote locations to pick up supplies from underground tunnels in places such as Africa and South America.

So then stuff is trucked in on the surface, taken down into these tunnels and then taken to some . . .

No. Well, yes, in a sense, yes. It's trucked in on the surface but there are also manufacturing capabilities beneath the surface. So you understand, think about it: underground cities. We're not just talking about residences and places where people sleep, we're also talking about heavy industrial manufacturing capabilities; and they could build airplanes down there easily.

At the Cape of Good Hope and these other places in South America and Africa that you mentioned or just at the Cape of Good Hope?

No. They could build in the underground base at the Cape of Good Hope and also at the bases near the North and South Poles. But the other bases, no, they don't have the heavy manufacturing capability there.

So there are three places on this planet where they can build airplanes, flying disks, submarines, anything they want to build?

Anything technologically, yes. They can build their own computers. All they need, essentially, are the raw materials. For the sake of expediency, they will occasionally obtain materials that are surface-created, but since they believe that the materials that they create are superior to the ones created on the surface, they try to avoid surface materials, especially when it comes to crystal components, which, for example, would be printed circuits. The circuits that they can make are, in fact, much better because they can make them in what are called neutral environments. For example, a neutral environment exists in space.

So they build their own space stations?

Yes, at manufacturing facilities, because many, many steps can be eliminated when you are functioning in those neutral environments. It's much cheaper.

So they have satellites? Are there satellites going around the world that are not our satellites?

Yes, and some of these satellites are quite large. I'd say the largest of them is about three and one-half miles long. Think about the manufacturing capabilities. Really, crews' quarters are the minimum. They are essentially factories in space.

Where is that large one?

It is in orbit, generally around the poles, North Pole, South Pole and so on. It derives its energy from tapping into the poles of Earth. And it does not discharge anything, meaning all waste products are recycled without exception. In this way they avoid detection. They can mask themselves, yes, but if you're leaving debris behind you, eventually people wonder where the stuff is coming from.

So it has the same optical illusion technology – we can't see it?

You can't see it, no. It's masked all the time. It can unmask if it is necessary to repair something or if it's necessary to make a show of itself but they haven't done it in the past 25 or 30 years.

How long has it been there?

It's been there now about 105 years. It was not built by the people, you know, in the underground bases, by Earth people. It was built by the ETs and brought here and considered . . . well, I don't want to say a bribe, but let's say a gift.

But that's 1890, so we're going back before what we had thought of as the beginning of the appearance of UFOs.

Yes. It was brought here. It wasn't actually occupied by – let's call them strategic forces of the Earth – until about 1943, 1944. But it was established in orbit, and those who brought it here established certain manufacturing capabilities when they were able to study the Earth, trends on the Earth, what would be needed and what they felt would be valued. They didn't put in all of the manufacturing. They put in some. And so they were doing that for several years but it wasn't actually occupied by surface Earth people of any form till the early to mid-forties.

So you're saying that before and during the Second World War, the shadow government-ET alliance was in effect?

Oh, yes. It was actually in effect well before that. It started around the 1890s. This is not to say the shadow government started then, but the shadow government-ET alliance started then.

Who were the ETs? From what culture, what place, what planet, what civilization? What would we call them? Zetas, Pleiadians, Orions? Who were the ETs who came to make this alliance?

Initially, a very small group of about nine people. Just a moment. I think we're dealing with X-P-O-T-A-Z again.

Oh, the Renegades who mine on the Moon were the first ones.

Yes.

So at that time, then, there was on the Earth a shadow government. They weren't allied with anybody but they sort of controlled the money and the resources behind the scenes. Is that what we can say?

Yes, they were not 100% in control at that time, meaning that in areas they had not fully explored they were not ruling with an iron fist, as it were, behind the scenes.

But they still controlled governments?

They controlled governments and they had influence. Although they were not 100% in control, they had about 80% control and were the significant influence in the U.S. government at that time. But they were not totally in control.

And what about the rest of the governments?

The U.S. government has always been a little easier to manipulate, but they had, at that time in the 1890s, about 20% control in China. This is not to say that other people were manipulated in the government in China, but that particular organization had about 20% in China. They had about 3% in India. Not much. They couldn't get a lot of control in India in the early days. And they had — let's see where else would you be interested in? They had about 17% in France.

Interestingly enough, France and India were the ones they had the most trouble with. India just has spirit energy, essentially, and it is hard for them to maintain control; even to this day they do not have 100% control in India. But France was also difficult because the people have an innate sense of going their own way, and this has benefited France greatly. At that time they also had about 40% influence in Great Britain, which was a significant colonial power then — definitely Great Britain.

I thought the Americans were the free spirits? How did we become puppets?

I don't know. As long as the white man has been here, this has always been a country in search of someone to look up to. That is part of the reason that the Christian religion — let's say the Judeo-Christian, but primarily the Christian religion — has taken root so strongly here; because the Christian religion by its very nature gives you more than one someone to look up to. There's someone for everyone in the family to look up to. It is less true with the Jewish religion, but it's there.

The Buddhist religion has not taken over this country and it never will. There will always be people who will follow it, but the Buddhist religion is not trying to give you leaders with absolute authority. It is trying to create a certain amount of autonomy in individuals. So, I would say that this country has been ripe for manipulation since the arrival of the white man.

I understand. An outside authority. Okay, so there was on Earth a group in 1890 that made an alliance with just eight or nine Renegades.

Yes, and you know, it's quite astonishing what can be done with automation. When the Renegades arrived, they weren't actually on that vehicle; they had that vehicle with the space manufacturing lab essentially in tow when they arrived. They arrived on a flying disk. But the nine people working with about 180 androids — I'm loathe, again, to use the word androids because they're more machine than flesh, but they are too advanced just to be called robots — created much of the exotic machinery that still today is light-years ahead of what can be produced even by the secret government. Of course, you can understand that a prize like this, a manufacturing facility that can produce things almost cosmically, is definitely valued.

The Renegades Kept the Secret of the Vehicle's Spiritual Fulfillment

I might add also that the individuals we've come to call the Renegades maintained a certain level of control over that vehicle and passed not all of the secrets of the control on to their heirs from Xpotaz, which I'm having difficulty pronouncing in your language. They did not pass that much of the wisdom on to the secret government or to any of what they would call Earth humans.

So it is interesting to note that even those original people from that place did not pass on all the secrets to their own heirs because the original Renegades had a greater connection to spirit forces, to God, if you would. And they believed that when their own people, their own heirs, had evolved sufficiently, they would be able to unlock the secrets of converting this vehicle into what it was originally intended to be, which is essentially a place of spiritual fulfillment. Meaning it has to become essentially the polar opposite of what it now is.

It is not unlike what human beings go through in the death cycle. When they release, no matter how negative they might be, they release all this negativity and convert themselves into what amounts to loving spirit-beings.

The ship, we have to understand, is essentially alive; it is ensouled and spiritized. Only this is not, even today, even remotely understood by the secret government of Earth and only negligibly understood by the descendants of the initial Renegades. So this puts a whole different point of view on who the Renegades are. When the

Renegades' heirs evolve a little bit more, which is probably going to take them about twenty years, they will discover the means by which to transform that ship. This cannot be done exactly by thought. I can't tell you how it can be done or I'll give it away. But it can be done remotely; that's essentially what I would say, and it can also be done in person. When they do that, not only will the ship transform, but, by necessity, so will the secret government begin to transform, because it's like the story about the hundredth monkey.

In this case, there will be people on board who are either influenced by or associated with the secret government. Anything on board that ship is going to transform when that ship transforms. They will be able to freely move amongst the people who are their associates and they will not appear transformed, nor will it be detectable in any way that they have changed. But they will know. And they will act essentially like an antiviral shot that the doctor gives you to protect you from a disease when they go to these bases even in their dreams, so they can't be prevented. When they interact with the people from whom they have sprung or to whom they are Source, they will essentially inoculate them and move them up more into their spirit-beings.

Who actually inhabits and works on this vehicle now? Are these created beings?

Well, we still have the original 180 androidal robots. The nine Renegades are no longer alive. They've all passed over, so we have a few, maybe two or three, of their descendants who are there. That's no more of them than are necessary; and there are about 150 to 180 personnel of the secret government, all Earth-surface people, not underground people.

Are these scientists, technical workers, slaves, laborers or what?

No, these are essentially scientists, people who are trained, not on the surface of the Earth, but trained in educational facilities located within the vehicle itself. The training does not occur in classes. It occurs individually by a method known as inculcation. This is not a cruel way to teach, but it is uncomfortable. You learn vast amounts in a very short amount of time, but it is a shock to the system.

Would you describe the process?

There are no drugs involved. It is that certain needles, not unlike acupuncture needles, attach to what you would call, if you looked at it, an electronic device, but there are no wires going to it. Then these things that look not dissimilar to earmuffs are clamped to the side of your head, including a couple of needles that go in around, well, right underneath your lower lip, around your jaw. It's not particularly comfortable, but it stimulates points that allow you to receive a tremendous amount of information and knowledge in a short time, after which you have to sleep. After one of these experiences, which lasts maybe five minutes at the most, you then have to sleep for about sixteen hours. You're exhausted, your body's organs have been fully tested to their limits and it takes sixteen hours just to recover physically. And I might add that emotionally you become very taut. That is not taken care of; only the body and the mind are addressed.

All right, so when did they start building the headquarters at Good Hope and the two at the poles? When did they actually physically start building those underground bases?

The ones at the poles were built around the 1920s. You understand that in the 1920s there weren't a whole lot of people around, so a significant amount of work could be done on the surface without detection. There were some native peoples there, but the native peoples just left them alone and did not go there. It was not necessary to put up any devices to deflect people. For one thing, they did not have the devices; for another thing, people just didn't need to go there. While something was going on there and they didn't know what, they stayed away because it didn't look safe or didn't feel safe. There was also the primary means by which human beings learn: The animals wouldn't go there. People who live in the wild know that if the animals don't go to a place, it's probably better that they not go there, either. So they were able to access it from the surface.

There were all the other groups that came in later and created alliances. When did that happen and who were those beings?

Are you talking about the alliance with the negative Sirians?

Well, there are the negative Sirians and then there are all the other ones — the Orions, the Pleiadians. Did they all come separately?

They came in separately. And you must understand that because of this initial experience with ETs, which, as far as I know, was the first contact of an authoritarian nature, when the others showed up, the secret government individuals had already essentially established a protocol for how to deal with them. So when these other ETs showed up, the shadow government realized they were going to have to give up certain things, but they would be able to get things in return. By keeping their agreements as secret as possible and knowing that many of the negative ETs were enemies of each other, they knew that if they played their cards right, they could become a significant power in their own right. One group of negative ETs wouldn't even know what another group of negative ETs was giving the secret government of the Earth. They wouldn't know what was going on.

Chronologically, who was in the first group, where did they come from, what did they want, what did they get?

Xpotaz was the first group.

But after them.

Next came the Orions.

When?

About 1910, initially.

And what did they want? How many of them were there? What did they give?

It was a very small group, no more than fifty. They wanted to be able to access randomly the people of Earth, not to take Earth people with them but to take over some Earth people's bodies. This was essentially something they had been able to do on other planets. But as it turned out, they were not able to do it here. For one thing, Earth people at that time lived on the surface, for the most part, and these negative Orion beings could not live on the surface of the Earth even if they were dominating another person's body, essentially possessing another person, because they would be affected by Earth energy. So this experiment essentially failed. Nevertheless, the secret government got some goodies. They said, sure, go ahead.

What did they get?

They got from them a very small device. You know, ETs will give you small things if they possibly can because that makes it difficult for you to take it apart and figure out what it does, especially when you don't have any idea what those little parts in there are. They gave them a very small device that would essentially be considered by today's standards a laser gun. It took the secret government a good thirty years to be able to duplicate it.

And what did they do with it? Is that part of the laser weapons system now?

Now it has essentially evolved through various generations into being the laser weapons systems that you have today.

Okay, so who came next and what did they want and what did they give?

Next, I believe we had some negative individuals from Sirius, of whom there are very few, I might add, so few they're infinitesimal in number in comparison to the positive individuals. But we had essentially a renegade group from Sirius. They came from a positive planet, but they were just renegades. They wanted to start an undersea base deep within the Pacific Trench where they would essentially conduct experiments attempting to tap the energy of the center of the Earth.

The secret government knows you can't say no to these people; the only thing you can do is to negotiate and try to get the most you can. So from those people they received advanced medical techniques: essentially, a chamber you can go into and all of your ills are corrected through, for lack of a better term, cosmic energy. However, to work, the device must have an antenna to the surface of the Earth pointed at the Sun. So, because of the nature of clandestine activities, the device was not freely utilized.

It was placed eventually aboard one of these submersible ships and is used sometimes. They've never been able to duplicate it, I might add.

The Sirian beings were unable to utilize the technology they had to tap the core energy of the Earth. They were able, however, to drain off a very small amount that Earth could spare. That's what they really wanted; they came here and they left.

What year was that?

It was about 1916. They were here for less than a year.

Then who?

Then I think we had, around the 1920s, people who were not as negative as what are called now the Grays. I'm not talking about the Zeta Reticulum beings, I'm talking about a subspecies of the Zeta beings. They came and they hung around; they didn't want that much. They were, as is the propensity with all beings from Zeta Reticulum or their genetic cousins, looking for genetic material, primarily, and did not want to kill or really maim anybody but wanted to gather genetic material at will from anywhere. They offered to the secret government, and they were the first ones to do this, the energy device that powers the flying disks. So that was the first major coup by the secret government.

I might add that all previous ETs who had come had realized that you could essentially give the secret government a trinket, from their point of view, and they would be happy. But these people, being unsophisticated, thought they had to give something big. So they were the first ones to give something big. You know the joke — they gave them the whole farm instead of a loaf of bread. That's really true, they did.

How many of these Grays came here?

Initially there were about 400. They came in a large vehicle; several smaller ships could enter and exit from it.

Are they still here?

They're still here, yes. Those original beings are all still here. They are still gathering genetic material, but not very much. The only people they gather it from now are people who have unusual genetic anomalies, Earth people with either naturally occurring anomalies or anomalies artificially created by them and other ETs interacting with Earth people.

Okay, we're up to the 1920s. But my question now is this: A few beings come from someplace to the planet. How do they do the take-me-to-your-leader bit? I mean, how do they know whom to talk to? How do they find this little tiny group of shadow government people?

Well, essentially the Xpotaz people function as an intermediary.

So the new arrivals would go to them and then the Xpotaz would lead them . . .

Yes, it was kind of like a commission. They would go to them and essentially ask for permission to pursue their interests on Earth. They would have to ask for permission because on board that vehicle the Xpotazes do have a time-beam weapon. It was, perhaps, the most secret device on that vehicle. It cannot be activated even to this day by the secret government, but it can be activated by the descendants of the original Renegades. A time-beam weapon does not uncreate anything. It does not destroy anything. But say you are sending an invading vehicle, from their point of view. They aim the time-beam weapon at it . . .

And take it to the year 1600 or something.

You don't just take it to the year 1600; you can transfer that vehicle to anywhere in the universe in any time, and the vehicle might never be able to find its way back. It is perhaps one of the most ruthless weapons, because the people can't even find their way home. The chances of finding your way home before you die are very small.

The reason they were acting as a very powerful intermediary, the reason the negative Orions, the negative Sirians, the Grays and so on went to them first to ask permission was that these people had the power to knock invading ships from other places out of the sky and into some other time, some other place. They had to go to them because if they tried to go directly to the secret government on Earth, they would be shot at. That did happen.

As is often the case with powerful, ruthless beings, an example was made initially. The beings known as the Grays had come here before that successful mission of about 400 individuals. There was a smaller mission of about nine who came in a flying disk, and they came directly toward the Earth. They were warned, in their own language, that if they attempted to approach the secret government without going through the intermediary of the Renegades and essentially bribing them, they would be placed somewhere else. They ignored it, and the time-beam weapon was used on them. I am sorry to say these beings are still lost in time in another place in the universe. They essentially were sent back about 500 million years into a place in the universe where even with the fastest of time travel they would not be able to get home to their own planet. It is not likely that they will be rescued in their lifetimes, and they have about another couple of hundred years to go. It is very sad for them.

Then the word got out, so after that, they all came to the intermediaries?

Yes.

Is that the weapon they are threatening the Earth with?

No.

Oh, that's just a small one.

They are claiming to the shadow government that they are protecting them with that weapon. The shadow government, however, is not foolish. They are crystal clear that this weapon could be used against them, so it does keep them a little bit in check; not totally, but a little bit.

So we're in the 1920s with the 400 Grays. At what point do these 400 go underground into one of the five bases?

They can, but they don't very often. They don't have to. The vehicle that holds their individual flying disks has sufficient capacity to take care of all their needs. It's essentially a small mothership.

Who came next?

After that, I don't think there was much more. We're only talking about negative beings here.

Allied with the shadow government.

That's all, as far as I can tell.

How did we get so many? Did they all have descendants?

Yes, of course, certainly.

In the 1920s we got the Grays. Then how do we get from there to these cities underground?

They had manufacturing that could go unfettered, with tremendously advanced technology, more advanced and up-to-date in the 1920s than what is on Earth now. When you start building these underground bases, if it goes unfettered with nothing stopping you and you have tremendous technology, you can do a lot in a small time. And if you know that you're going to be using it later, that you're going to have an underground city with lots and lots of people doing lots and lots of things, you build that city right then and there, using material that does not decay.

So if it's made on the spaceship, it doesn't wear out and decay?

The manufacturing instruments used to build these houses used an incredibly small amount of a material that comes from other planets. Can you imagine bulldozing that much rock? What do you do with rock that has almost as much bulk as Rhode Island? That's a lot of rock.

You fuse it. You melt it and fuse it.

No, no. Even if you fuse it, you still have mass. What do you do with it? Where does it go? You use it to make *everything* you're making, so nothing is wasted. Never forget, when it comes to recycling, the secret government is no slouch, to use your term. They used it all, along with an infinitesimal amount of material from another planet that allows the material to remain in that shape without any perceptible decay once it is built, created or formed. In about 50,000 years it will be worn out, but that's a long time.

So it becomes almost like the rock it was created from?

Yes, it has a certain immortal aspect to it.

So they built houses, shopping centers, hospitals, they built everything you'd have in a city.

Not shopping centers as you know them, but they built entertainment places. Understand, they're not trying to get people too involved in their private lives.

Well, they don't have private lives, then. Do the ETs have their dependents with them? Do they have wives and children? They must, if they're procreating and expanding.

Most of the procreation is done through cloning with the ETs. Those who wish to have contact with families as you understand the word, are, how can we say, discreet enough to know that it would be a big mistake to have those families right there on a base with the secret government. So they don't. They go to their motherships to have their R&R because you're not going to want to bring your family to a place where they can be used against you by people who cannot be trusted.

Okay, that's why these bases are totally and absolutely male. So, in the 1920s they began to build them; when would you say they were completed?

Of course, the initial underground cities were not as numerous as they are today, so let's just say that the North Pole and the South Pole bases were fully completed in their initial stages by 1928. And by 1938, they were built up into what they are today, not including all the technological machinery, but essentially all that is needed to keep many different groups of people sufficiently sustained.

When did they build the underground installation under Secret Canyon?

I think that was done mostly in the 1940s for its initial stage. Yes, it's been expanded now and then, but the primary base was built in the '40s as a small outpost. It was not because there were Earth humans here that they were particularly interested in; it was because the energies of the place were strong then. Of course, because of various disruptions underground since, and because of competition for underground space, they're probably going to shut that base down before too long. It is here also because the energy the planet has to provide to this area radiates through her stone antennas to other planets. She is having to use so much energy just to maintain her structural integrity because of all the tunnels and so on being built through her flesh — and her stone is her flesh — that they're probably going to shut down that base within the next three, four, five years at the most. They'll probably leave an outpost, but that's it.

What do they do there? Is it the flying saucer headquarters?

That's one way to put it, yes. But they'll move it. They have been moving it, in any event, because there are so many people here now and detection is something that is happening almost every day by casual bystanders. It's just getting to be a security nightmare. They don't need the struggle.

So they're moving it from the Sedona area. Do they have a place to take it to?

Yes. They already have a place that is masked in plain sight. That's where they're going to go. They're going to move it a considerable distance when measured in nautical miles — I'm giving you that hint.

What is the purpose of the Sedona base? It's a headquarters for the flying disks, but what else do they do there?

They do long-range research on human characteristics and behavior — behavioral analysis — with the intention of controlling, manipulating and conserving certain behaviors they can use to their benefit. It's a psychological as well as a scientific group. It's a chemical, organic, as well as a psychological place.

Energy Manipulations in Sedona

They are involved in experiments, and this is part of the reason that people are energetically manipulated somewhat in Sedona. When people in Sedona feel the energies radiating from Mother Earth, they feel great. But when there are whole days or weeks when everybody you know is feeling awful, totally upset, there is a beam weapon being directed toward you to observe how even the best of friends, lovers, family members can become estranged. They are not trying to cause crime in the streets; they want to see how far they can push people into negative patterns of behavior, and it can be tested only on people who are at other times peacefully and benevolently living together.

So how do they observe this, then? What techniques of observation do they have?

They have people here amongst you, and they can simply read the police reports. They also have a means of reading your thoughts. Interestingly enough, they do not have a means of reading your feelings, nor do they consider your feelings to be that important. It's part of the reason they can be so ruthless. But on the other hand, that also does not allow them to develop true power, which is associated with feelings. They can't develop that in any event, because they would have to get more into their own feelings, which would necessarily transform them.

But you will, in time, transform them through how you feel, not through what you think; they cannot be transformed that way. You can transform them through what you feel, and you can use your thoughts to stimulate and support those feelings. It will be the feelings that will transform them.

They don't want us to go into the fourth dimension, so aren't they doing experimental work on astral bodies, trying to figure out how to control the next level?

Yes.

They themselves, in those underground bases, have the ability to operate as a point of Light, or they have abilities we don't have.

Not a point of Light. Let's not call it a point of Light. *A point of energy,* how's that?

Okay, but they can come and go without their physical bodies and they can observe, they can manipulate, they can do many, many things. ·

Some of them. Let's say some of them have sorcery abilities. But they do not have the powers of, say, a true Lightbeing, a loving Lightbeing. Sorcery cannot have those powers. It is, by its true nature, not allowed to, because many of the things that happen at the loving levels of Light — the creation, the allowance — they cannot do because they are so dense. Now, when I say dense, I am not talking about physically dense; I am talking about spiritually dense. They are necessarily limited by the means they use to manipulate others. This is good.

Underground Bases and the Secret Government

Zoosh through Robert Shapiro
August 2, 1994

We know that for 300,000 years this planet has been controlled by *negative beings. That's what this war in the heavens was just about. The Lightbeings, to my understanding, took back control of it. So these two Xpotazes and nine Renegades and so forth are here because the men who run the secret government have always been allied with extraterrestrials. Proceed with that and then we'll get some details.*

That's how they've always been able to be one step ahead of the game, while other people, perhaps on some opposing or simply competing side, would have their best guess as to what the secret government would do. The secret government actually had alliances with people who can travel in time and get a prediction of what would happen based upon almost total accuracy. So if you know absolutely what your competitor is going to do, the need to get one up on them is considerably eased. So yes, the shadow government has always been in alignment with extraterrestrials who always wanted something from Earth, sometimes from the secret government itself, sometimes from the people of Earth, sometimes even from — and this is perhaps the most important — sometimes from the *future* of Earth.

So you have to understand that at the very beginning when this first started, the secret government — those who were behind the scenes then — essentially mortgaged the future of Earth and its people so that the inheritors of that secret government authority were absolutely bound to previously made contracts. Even if they wanted to extricate themselves and change things to become more moderate, they did not have the opportunity. They were essentially manacled with the contracts that were already sealed. Contracts like that are not something that are renegotiated. They are sealed and that's it! It's like, well, we'll do this for you and you do that for us. And then there will be certain givens on the other side. If either one of us does this, then you can do that and so on.

So let's give those in power in the secret government a certain amount of forgiveness, for most of them have inherited things. They were born into a situation that existed. People in the secret government are essentially born into their jobs. They do not go out and play catch and baseball much when they are youngsters. When they are three and four years old they are already being taken to the chambers of power so they can see and be trained and programmed with an attitude about themselves that has to do with service, believe it or not, and primarily with selflessness. This is how they are able to maintain their secretiveness about who they are. For after all, if they were interested in material wealth, they would become prominent, they would become known, they would certainly attract attention.

But they do not. Why not? Because they are trained to service and selflessness to promote the Association, as it is called sometimes, and also to learn the value of invisibility, or blending into the surroundings. It's hard to imagine the secret government being selfless, but most of the people truly are. If they have any wealth, then it is associated with some other aspect of their position. But many of them are anonymous people, people who would be lost in a crowd of three people.

The Origin of the Secret Government: Atlantis, Lucifer and Light Skins

When did that alliance start? What period in our history and with whom?

Really, it was a little further back. It was close to half a million years ago when it first started. Well, if we actually take it back all the way, it started with Atlantis, because those that started Atlantis were actually working with what was then a more angelic version of Lucifer. And you could say that Lucifer, being an extraterrestrial, of course, unintentionally began the secret government because he was the first extraterrestrial who had contracts with people associated with Earth, albeit at a different vibration. But it was during Atlantis that the vibration began moving toward the third dimension. So you could say that it began way back then.

Put a date on that — 750,000, 800,000 years ago?

Yes, something like that is as close as we can get, allowing for the change in dimension. Yes, around then. So that was actually the first point of being, although of course Lucifer also got densified in that process. Before he knew it, he was tied in and had to become something other than what he had planned. But we have discussed this before.

To put a modern light on when the contract got going, it was about half a million years ago. It was then that people looking like yourselves with light-colored skin began to be a force to reckon with on this planet. Light-colored people have been here for about a million years, no more than that. One is not always a light-colored person; one goes through all these different skin tonations as well as appearances. But it is interesting that in races there are genetic lessons, and the genetic lesson of the light-colored people is adaptability. However, as one understands lessons, one must understand that when adaptability is the lesson, there is resistance to that lesson. The form that resistance would take is the desire to control, to be in charge.

Since they were not a force to be reckoned with for half a million years or so, they were picked on by everybody else. Because they were low in the pecking order, they cried out for people from their cultural heritage — this was the key: in any form — to come and help them. So people from Orion, from its more violent past, came in the form of these people and this created the first alliances. Now, that alliance lasted only a few hundred years and then things got shaken up. Then it reestablished itself about 350,000 years ago, again with the light-skinned people, because remember, the light-skinned people are learning how to adapt. An interesting sidelight here: When light-skinned people get a tan, they are learning how to adapt, because the natural skin tone associated with this planet, even before any human beings were here of any race, was darker — naturally because of the Sun.

This would be Orions again, then, 350,000 years ago?

Yes. It was quite a while before the negative-polarized people from that small planet in Sirius showed up. They were not a major force to be reckoned with because they simply did not have the sophistication to get here. When Jehovah left on the big ship from that negative planet [Sirius], being a positive being, he took with him all his people, who were technocrats, including Lucifer, even though they knew that he had some leanings at that time toward being corruptible or corrupting others. They couldn't afford to leave him behind, because if they had, he would have immediately organized a search party to find them. He also would have organized people to achieve technical superiority that would have been used to exploit others. They couldn't afford to leave him behind, so they took him with them.

Okay, what year was that?

Again, we're talking about different dimensions, but as close as we can get, it is about a million and a half years. But it fluctuates; tomorrow I'd say two and a half million because *you* are moving in time.

So that's the first time we ever got a date for when the Explorer Race began — a million and a half years ago; then we jumped to Atlantis when . . .

You had a Lemurian-type civilization where people would receive and give on the basis of color, tone, feeling, and so on. Interchange was on the basis of that totally feminine means of being. When Lucifer arrived with Jehovah, Jehovah tended to go along with that method and the whole experiment. When Lucifer left Sirius, he explored with Jehovah and many others, and he didn't like the way things were done on Lemuria.

You must remember that Lucifer at that time was one of the rare beings who was almost totally polarized to the masculine. Lucifer was the product, in his original physical self, of a mixed marriage. This was unusual on Sirius at that time, even on a planet that was rigidly controlled. His father was from Orion, so he was an extraterrestrial in the context of Sirius. His mother was also an outcast, a product of Orion and Sirius. Thus Lucifer was born with a lot of Orion connection. So while everybody else tended to have sort of a gentleness about them (easily led and so on) even with the strident energy of that negative planet, Lucifer had a strong, strident way about him. So you can see where he'd be butting heads all the time with Jehovah.

Lucifer came down and he didn't like Lemuria. Too passive, he said (the type of comment you'd expect from him then, but not now). He started talking to some of the people out of Lemuria, the younger people who were still young enough to be influenced. (Lucifer has always been very influential. Even today he can definitely sell coal in Newcastle, as they say.) He talked them into experimenting. He said he would show them another island where they could run things for themselves. They could do what they want; he would give them the tools and show them how things could be done. Well, of course, once he gave that little speech, he committed himself to them and at the same time broke ties with Jehovah. That's how Atlantis got started. And of course the human beings in Lemuria who started it initially, started very much a Lemurian situation. It took generations for them to gradually let go of creating and providing what they needed through color, tone and feeling into having to do it slowly and build with tools and use genetics and the whole business. When you have a society like that, it inevitably tends to destroy itself, usually through some innocuous, unexpected plan. Occasionally it is destroyed through what amounts to Earth's antibodies, which is essentially her weather changes.

Keep going.

When Lucifer did that, he unintentionally started the shadow government. Here he was, clearly an extraterrestrial at a higher dimension of Earth, planting ideas that he thought were right. He wasn't saying, oh, how can I corrupt these people. At that time he wasn't like that. He just had his own way of doing things, and he wasn't satisfied with going along. (He could never go along. Now he can, but then he could not.)

The Origin of Science and Thinking

Lucifer essentially initiated Atlantis. He encouraged people to think. They didn't know how to think, so he initiated the idea of people thinking and accomplishing things through thought. No one had done that in Lemuria before because they didn't need to. They could think, but it was something for entertainment. So he got them started. He started working with them after he was outcast from Jehovah and Jehovah's ship. They gave him a small ship to take with him, and small ships have quite a bit of stuff. He showed them how they could create what they needed through science. Of course, being the godfather of these people, he became their leader during his lifetime. He showed them all he knew about science, which was considerable, but of course he could not teach them moral principles he had been taught. For one thing, he wasn't comfortable with them, and when he tried to teach it, his anger and discomfort with these moral principles would come through stronger than the words. And the people, remember, were still feeling, so they were feeling this much stronger than his words. They felt anger, distrust, discomfort with moral principles. So they, being essentially blank slates, are going to feel that moral principles do not apply to science. And that science is its own wondrous thing and needs to have no restrictions placed on it whatsoever.

You can see where this could lead to trouble, mischief. It did. They created a whole race of beings to do their labor for them. Why should we go dig, pick up stuff, when we could create these beings? How will we keep them happy? How do we keep them from revolting? Oh, let's see, maybe we can drug them. Give them some kind of drug they will like. It will make them work hard and they won't live very long, but for a reward we'll give them some other drugs, keep them drugged and happy. We'll give them whatever kind of food they want to eat. If they die young, it's okay because after all, we created them, so they're not really people.

That's how that whole idea started. I'm not saying that's true; what I'm saying is that it was their rationale.

That was their mentality.

That's how science became godless. Before that, science was sacred. All these things Lucifer started inadvertently. And when he died an old man, after his life Jehovah had a little talk with him. They had not seen each other in a long time. Jehovah said, "My friend, see what you have wrought?" Jehovah showed him the future, and Lucifer was genuinely sorry. He said, "I didn't realize that I was feeling that strongly rebellious against moral principles." Jehovah said, "I know that. But now you must stay to the end. And I, loving you like a brother, will stay with you. We won't live in the same places, but we will visit from time to time and talk. And I will show you the future so you can see it. For I will give you this much," Jehovah said, "I will give you my glimpse of the future so that when you are dragged down and must serve people's subconscious desires, which you unintentionally put on them, I will always show you the future. No matter how cynical or depraved you might become as a result of what you have begun here unintentionally, you must still live the consequences of your act; and I will show you the future. Sometimes the things I show you you won't like, and you will feel bad. You know that you will be in the middle of it and will have to be something you are not. But I will also show you the far future where things get better. If you can just get through these hard times, then things will be resolved and you will be the wiser for it." Lucifer said, "All right. I can get through it if you are here. But don't go." And Jehovah said, "All right."

Jehovah took some responsibility too, because he remembered that he had brought Lucifer with him for his own reasons. He could not afford to leave him behind. So Jehovah took responsibility for his actions and that is why he, Jehovah, stayed.

Atlantis and the Dimensional Split

Carry it forward a little bit so that people reading this can connect that to the secret government. So we had civilizations and governments and they'd blow themselves up. How did that work from the end of Atlantis?

When Atlantis ended, Atlantis didn't blow itself up so much as just stopped. It was like suspended animation. There were things going on with crystals. They were very influential; they were traveling in space — practicing a little mischief in space. They couldn't actually interfere with the extraterrestrials in space, but the extraterrestrials could defend themselves (for they were not allowed to be offensive). One way to defend yourself is to reflect back all that is being done to you, so they reflected back all that was being done. Thus the energy in Atlantis got more and more intense. Since the people there were using crystals to control, to create, to amplify everything, suddenly things started getting more and more powerful, more intense. And things were happening that they didn't like.

Then a group of people started working with crystals around the entire island in an attempt to bring the island into greater balance with the sea, for it was always considered that as long as the island and the energies of the island were compatible with the energies of the sea, they would be all right. But it wasn't working that way. They were starting to have earthquakes and so on, and they knew something was wrong. In the process, they linked all the crystals to uncreate their situation and recreate a balance with the sea. Well, the sequence, as often happens, is that their plan would essentially uncreate all of their existence and then have a programmed situation where it would recreate in more balance. They did not know that dimensions were shifting because of all this energy. So they actually achieved what they attempted to do. They uncreated their existence, all right, but the recreation took place at a higher level. And that higher level of Atlantis was more in line with a Lemuria. It exists today around the fifth or sixth dimension of Earth. *They think they succeeded;* they haven't got a clue that they left behind, in the third dimension of Earth, the shambles of what was Atlantis and a few bits and pieces left over in the sea of outposts of Atlantis. But there they went, and they had success. It's really ironic.

So that was the end of Atlantis as you know it in the third

dimension. But in the fifth and sixth dimension it's still fine. It's still there, and so is Lemuria.

Who's populating it, then? Is there a part of ourselves up there?

Not really. It's just as with all cases; the souls incarnate, pass over, reincarnate and so on. By now there are other souls occupying it, which is Creator's desire so that they will be compatible with Lemuria. Lemuria is still creating things, as always. And providing, receiving — all of this has always taken place. Now Atlantis is not using tools of manipulation whatsoever, but since it has its own unique desire, which is to learn how to create and uncreate on a more individual basis, the people on Atlantis are essentially one notch behind. The people in Lemuria are *doing* it; the people in Atlantis are *learning* how to do it. It's kind of interesting: It's as if the people from Lemuria left and could only take a step backwards, but they did not know that. So now Atlantis is the place where people learn how to do what people do naturally on Lemuria. This allows the Atlanteans to fulfill their original intent without causing any harm.

All right. So now we have the remnants of Atlantis. The people from Atlantis went to South America, Egypt, Spain, they went all over the planet, right?

The people? You mean the survivors? The survivors re-imaged themselves into the fifth and sixth dimensions. There were no survivors on the island. The only ones who survived had gone out earlier or were on missions or at outposts and so on.

But some people knew what was going to happen and they sent out some of their people and some of their artifacts and some of their teachers . .

Yes. There were some people in what amounted to anthropological outposts as well on other continents, yes.

So they were the beginning of the next round of civilization.

Yes. And already the foundation was laid to have allies from other planets.

Talk about that.

Lucifer had been from another planet. He was revered — and appreciated — at that time not as a god but as a master teacher. And also somewhat feared, as students tend to fear their teacher. But at that time the fear was not necessary. They were informed of what was going to be done. Later, in following generations, they realized what had happened and they went back. There was no island, nothing; they assumed that it had gone wrong — a reasonable assumption, from their point of view.

Here they were, shifting dimensions, you know, and they felt something was different because their bodies felt different. They knew something had happened, but they thought it was all a result of failed experiments on Atlantis. They did not realize that the experiment actually worked, but they were left behind. So then they set about trying to establish colonies. At that time they were a little more physical. They were now in third dimension and by then had discovered they were a little more physical and could be more easily injured. The tools they had with them, even crystal tools, need to be replenished somewhat from the main crystals that were focused from Atlantis, but they were not getting replenished. So eventually these crystals simply became the equivalent of Earth crystals, of third dimension, you understand. So they could not really do that much. Since they did not know how to use the crystals in a spiritual way and were essentially using them as tools, the crystals eventually became like rocks.

So there they were. They had to make the best of it. All their scientific knowledge, all their genetic knowledge did not help them. They had these little kits with them. They had been expecting to go back, you know, and were just out there for a short time. Eventually they used up their supplies, so they had to adapt. They still had, though, the fall-back position where they knew they could ask for help from anyplace. They were sending out, "Anybody, I don't care, someone come and help me." That's always a hazard. That would be their prayers for help. Well, since life was a little more tough then, they didn't all survive. But a few of them were able to take root.

Now we're coming into more modern times. They had two outposts at the very southern tip of the continent, now known as South Africa, one on the west coast and one on the east coast. The east coast outpost was a weather station and the west coast version was an anthropological expedition. The east coast weather station did not survive. One person escaped, but all the instruments were ruined. The survivor made it by foot to the west coast over several months, and on arrival was in a considerably bedraggled condition. He told them what had happened, and they immediately decided they'd have to go underground. The planet was hostile, there was no way of surviving, even though they were in touch with some of their other outposts, because their crystals no longer had any energy. They didn't know how to stay in touch telepathically. Remember, they were totally tool-oriented. They decided they had to have some help.

They did not trust the surface of the planet; they wanted to get underground, because it would be predictable. "We know what to expect, and while it won't be easy, once we get started, we'll be all right."

So again they prayed. They didn't realize their power. Being the students and descendants of Lucifer, who was still around, their prayers were relayed through Lucifer. Lucifer, being at least three-fourths associated with Orion, put it out there to his own sources.

You're saying that Lucifer somehow went to the third dimension?

Yes. Lucifer went to the third dimension, but he was in spirit. Remember, Jehovah said Lucifer had to stay with him through the whole thing.

Oh, he was in spirit.

He's there in spirit to help his children, as it were, and he's relaying the message to the only source that he knows can help them, which all gods-in-training do. Of course, here was a god-in-training who didn't realize he was going to be a negative god, as it were. He'd had a glimpse from Jehovah, but he was resisting it, so he went and passed the prayers on up the line. The message went to Orion, which sent a big ship. Another sidelight: The big ship arrived in two weeks, and Lucifer immediately went to the main deck. Although he was in spirit, he hoped that they could see him, identify him, and return his spirit to Orion so he could escape this terrible duty where he had to become, essentially, Satan. He hoped to escape.

But they did not see him. They were not that spiritually evolved, you understand. When he had asked for the Orion ship to come, it was not only to help his descendants, as it were, but himself. When they couldn't see him, Lucifer became angry. That's when he really got angry with Jehovah, became disappointed, and that's when he started feeling spiteful for the first time in his life. That's what "helped" him to descend to the level of Satan, his dark side — for Satan is Lucifer's dark side. You must understand that; Lucifer does have a light side.

The South African Base

So the ship came and the people on the west coast of southern South Africa felt they'd been saved. The ship looked over the planet, and they didn't see too much they were interested in, a little spot here and there where they could gather up a few minerals that might be of use to them, but they could get those anywhere. They felt like, so what? The ship was there for a few days before the people even knew about it. They saw it in the sky, but they didn't make any contact. But they had traveled in time, so while they were there, they surveyed the future of Earth. Is there anything here we're going to want? They looked at the past: no. They looked at the future, the immediate future: no, nothing there. Then they started looking way into the future, not just for themselves but for succeeding generations, for they were loyal to their own kind. And they started to see all the people; they started to see the needs of their own culture in the future who would require certain elements, certain metals and even, to some extent, water, particularly seawater. They didn't need that at that time, but they might need it in a hundred thousand, two hundred thousand, even three hundred thousand years in the future.

So they said, "Well, this is what we'll do. We'll help these people out. They want to be underground, we can make an underground base." So with their advanced technology they made an underground base that would be good for the people on the west coast of South Africa, the southernmost coast. The base was designed to be expanded into over the years so they themselves and their descendants could use it. In other words, they made a huge underground base that would be good for many, many, many thousands of years into the future. They gave these people technology, but they used the people. *That was always their intention.* Now, I'm not talking about Orions of today or Orions from a benevolent civilization. These are Orions who are not just negative, but let's say they're warriors — that puts it in a different context. Now, they approach the people, all smiles, you know, "How can we help you? We are here to help you," as the rescue ship approached them. "Oh, thank you so much for coming in answer to our prayers. We'd love to live underground. The surface of this planet is hostile; we can't survive on it. Many of our outposts have suffered. What can we do?"

"We will help you." "Thank you so much, thank you."

"We will build you a huge underground base." "Oh, we don't need very much space," the people said, "just a little underground base, no bigger than a square mile."

"Oh, but we would like to join you." "Oh, you would join us and help us?"

"Oh, yes, we would be glad to do that." (People on Earth were very naive even then.)

And so they hollowed it out; they didn't build the whole thing, but they created the space. Like I said, the base is just about as big as Rhode Island, underneath the southern tip of South Africa.

So there they were and they created this huge base. They didn't fill it all up with stuff; they made a place for them to access it. They knew that there was no reason for them to get highly involved here because their civilization was not going to need anything from Earth for a hundred thousand, two hundred thousand, even three hundred thousand years in the future. But they made a space to last. And they also gave themselves a servicing port there where they could come. They used these people as an excuse and said, "We will do all this for you, but we want your absolute guarantee that you will allow us free access to this planet at any time, not only now but in the future." And innocents abroad, as they were, said, "Absolutely. And how can we be certain of this?"

The Genetic Contract with the Orions

"Well," said the ET visitors, "if we make a genetic contract" — these people understood genetics, remember — "if we put something into your genetics that says you will defer to us when we have our needs and we put something into our genetics that says we will defer to you when you have your needs, then that would be the perfect contract. Then all succeeding generations on this planet, as you spread out and become more powerful — which you will, we'll see to that," say the ETs, "then we will defer to your needs and you will defer to our needs. It is a perfect contract, is it not?" "Oh yes, a wonderful contract, thank you."

Of course, they programmed the people on Earth to defer to *their* needs, but they faked the thing for themselves. And they could do it, with their superior technology. So that's how that contract got started.

So then what? How long did that ship stay here? They left?

That ship left, yes. It stayed about three or four weeks. It took them all of about sixteen hours to produce the space.

Of the size of Rhode Island?

That's right, underneath that particular part of Earth. And I can tell you, Earth didn't like it too much. And then they left a considerable amount of supplies. Every single one of the supplies they left, including things that would be consumed, had genetic transmitters. So if someone ate it, they would have a genetic transmitter that would lodge in some part of their body so that the people would always be trackable. In this way the Orions managed to get these transmitters inside most of the people. How'd they do that? Put it in the seeds. Genetic tracing. Even today, in your courts, you are dealing with genetic tracing. "How did we know the man was there? Well, we found his genetics there. We found a scraping, a piece of hair. He was there." I can assure you today that's not a surefire thing, just as an aside. Genetic tracing today is about 60% accurate at best. In the future, perhaps in another hundred years or so, it will be 100% accurate, but it isn't now.

But the ETs had 100% accuracy, so they were able to genetically induce a control factor on the peoples on Earth for all succeeding generations — and, I might add, on animals to some extent, because animals would eat, too. So they were able to go back to their planet and say, look, we've got something for you. It's no good now, but in the future it'll be great.

Anybody on that Orion ship with a name that is part of our culture? Part of our myths or legends?

It is important, but I don't know if I can tell you. I'll tell you a few. But again, we're taking a chance at offending people. That's how it is. Thoth was one of those beings who came to do good things. Later he also took the form of Quetzalcoatl. Quetzalcoatl was the descendant of the original Thoth from that ship. As a descendant, he naturally did not feel good about those original decisions and hence tried to do the opposite, to do the best he could for the people on Earth. This is part of the reason he went into medicine and healing. What else do you want to talk about?

The whole genetic coding, I guess.

The Orions had altered the Atlanteans' genetics so they would have a built-in desire to serve the Orions' needs. Though they had agreed to a similar alteration of their own genes to serve future Atlanteans' needs, they did not do so. They had superior technology, of course, and faked it. And then they left. They had built the whole underground base about the size of Rhode Island.

Of course, the Earth people at that time needed only a small portion of that space. The Orions set up part of the space for themselves, masking part of the space so that the people, who were Earth Atlanteans, could not see it clearly. It would be like looking at a hazy mirror. And they said, "It's probably not safe for you to go past this point because this is where we keep mechanisms for our personal atmosphere, for our personal nurturance, fuel for our craft, which is highly toxic. So don't go past this point."

They also set it up in such a way that as people approached

from a distance of about a hundred feet, they started to feel sick. They would say, "Well, this is taboo, we don't go there." And of course, in that place they put in a lot of their machinery to control things, to manufacture the genetic trace that would go into all things —seeds, food, equipment, everything they had provided for these people, everything they encouraged people to spread out over the surface of the Earth, so that anybody who would eat or use anything they left here would be encoded genetically with a willingness to serve their needs —even though they had no idea whether this would ever be used.

It was an investment on their part. After all, they personally, would never live to see the investment utilized in any way. They didn't even know whether it would be approved of when they got back home. They took a chance, essentially. Having looked at the future, they took a chance that their future generations would come to Earth, would utilize Earth's resources, Earth's people, Earth's energies, and most importantly, the seawater. Seawater would be useful to them in future generations because they could use it as a fuel. They wouldn't need very much of it, which is why you don't notice it missing. So that is what they did.

They went back to Orion and they said, "Is it all right? Did we exceed our authority?" And their people said, "Well, we use precious resources and it's obviously not something we can use right now." They replied, "Well, we hoped it would be all right since it will be needed in the future." And they were told, "It's all right. We know you did what you felt was best. You were there and you had to make a decision, so that was it." And then the people on Orion went on with their lives. It wasn't until another 150,000 years or so that they took up where they left off and showed up.

Other Outposts; A Lemurian Genetic Code

Let's backtrack a bit: There were people in other Atlantean outposts, and those people were initially helped by others. But let's say this: The original Orions, negative Orions as you call them, but really warrior Orions as I call them, did not return. And nobody from that culture returned from out of the past, present or future. Nobody from that culture returned to the planet for about 100,000 to 150,000 years in Earth time. However, when other groups of Atlantean beings cried out for help and there was no response, they had to learn how to get along. Some of them got along and formed the basis for certain tribes, or united with other tribes and got along the best they could. Some survived, some didn't. But *their* genetic code has come into your generation. They were originally Lemurian, anyway, from their genetic code.

Now what about the base in Iceland? There was an outpost group at the Ice, as they would call themselves, going to the Ice, and they lived in a small shelter. They also cried out for help, but in this case they did not receive help initially from negative peoples. They received help from more benevolent beings, from the adventurist Pleiadians. The Pleiadians and also some positive Sirians came there and helped them out. They also gave them an underground base, but they did not hollow anything out. They found an underground cavern. They asked, spiritually, whether Mother Earth would volunteer this cavern, which was not occupied by any physical or spiritual life form. Mother Earth said, okay. So they set up a small culture that began to recycle almost everything and could sustain itself. They gave only the instruments that would help sustain themselves, a small unit that created an artificial sun by which the people could produce crops underground, could have a life, and would have sufficient room for offspring in succeeding generations as long as they maintained a balance and did not expand their population too much. They couldn't really expand past the point of 2000 people; the cavern was that big.

So they started benevolently. Then they said goodby, not needing any contracts or anything from people of Earth, "Goodbye, we're glad to have helped you." The Earth Atlanteans said, "Thank you so much; we never could have done it without you." They were there for maybe a year or two. "Now you can make it on your own," said the ETs, and off they went.

So in succeeding generations, eventually 150,000 years down the line, along came the negative Orions to the Atlanteans. They discovered this base, and they said, "What a wonderful outpost for us. How can we influence these people? Here they are, living a fairly idyllic life, what do they need from us?" The more positive, protecting ETs had already pulled back from the planet because they realized something was going on that they could not protect the planet from, some kind of experiment with polarity. So the negative Orions, about 150,000 years ago from your point of time, said, "How can we bring these people into our fold? They don't need a thing from us. They've got everything they need, they're in a relatively protected spot. But they do have a weak point," someone noticed. "And that weak point is that they have an opening to the surface. How can we help them?" They think on it for a while, and they think, "We can help them if we can create a diversion where they *think* they are being threatened from outer space and then we rescue them. We won't even wait for them to ask for help. We'll rescue them and then we'll show up like the good guys and we'll say, 'Oh, we have helped you.' That's how we'll be able to get in with these people."

So that's what they did. They took a couple of their ships, masking them to make them look like something other than what they normally were, and sent them out robotically with none of their people inside. The ships attacked the area. They did some damage, nothing serious, nothing that they could not repair with the equipment they had. The weapons were fired specifically at places they had the capacity to repair. Then they came along and shot down the ships, saying, "We are here, we have helped you." The people said, "Oh thank you, thank you. We didn't have any means to defend ourselves. What would we have done without you?" One thing led to another. That's how they got a base in Iceland.

All right, so somehow this has to come forward where we get a shadow government. How does that evolve?

Remember that everything was encoded with this genetic transmitter seed, as it were.

So they did that to the Iceland base, too?

Yes, they did.

150,000 years ago?

Present Stimulation of the Genetic Device

Yes, they did that, but also they wanted to spread this stuff around on the surface of the planet so that succeeding generations would have that genetic coding. They'd only have to do it at a certain point, knowing then that very few ETs would be coming to colonize the planet. All they had to do was get into one generation, and whoever survived in that generation would pass it on to succeeding generations. So that's what they did. Up to the present time, there are certain foods that are more hazardous because they feed this device inside you, which is essentially dormant, and give it a little energy.

Coffee, chocolate . . .

. . . liquor, television. Television broadcasts a lot of excessive energy. Understand that they throw rays up to and through the tube and keep on going. That's why the tubes always have static electricity. It creates a lot of problems, but we won't talk about that now. I'll simply say this: Essentially, that dormant device is stimulated and made to work better by anything that feeds it. The molecule associated with sugar is almost exactly the same molecule associated with alcohol — any molecules like that. So there would be sugar, alcohol, or *anything having to do with latent static electricity or ELF*. Television produces extra-low-frequency energy (it is a byproduct, not intentional) and also static electricity. If you've ever seen the experiment with a Van de Graaff generator in high school physics class, a person puts his hand on the generator, which produces 100,000 volts; his hair stands up, but it doesn't hurt him because it's not producing any amps. That's an extreme case of static electricity. It makes you nervous, makes you feel uncomfortable. It also activates that device. When that device is activated, what happens to you? You become polarized one of two ways: Either you get warriorlike or you become subservient, but nothing in between. So you can be manipulated because you're being subservient, or you can be commanded as a warrior. You don't become a general or an admiral, you become a soldier.

It seems very complicated, but it can be very easily nullified. How, you say? It can be nullified by coming into your heart-feeling space. That's why it does not affect the animals even though they have been impregnated with it. Animals function from their heart-feeling space, some more than others. Deer, for example, are in their heart-feeling space all the time, so the dormant device within their genetic code does not affect them at all. Most animals come from this space. Plants, too, are coming from this space, so they are not affected. Only some genetically altered plants can be affected because they lose their original soul. If they lose their identity, they can be affected.

What *you* can do is be more in your heart space. When you are there, interesting things happen. As long as you stay in your heart space, which is not a mental thing, then you are in a more spiritual space. You can eat ice cream, drink coffee, eat chocolate and watch TV, and it doesn't affect you at all. The device remains dormant.

But that would be like a test. You go to see the guru and you have all these attitudes about things. Sitting next to the guru is a bottle of liquor and a bowl of candy. You look at these things and say, "What is that there for? My great guru, this great teacher, he would never drink liquor, he would never eat candy." And yet, the guru is in that heart space, takes a drink of liquor and eats chocolate, looks at you and smiles. Does that mean you're supposed to drink liquor and eat chocolate? You know that whenever you drink liquor and eat chocolate, you go nuts. No, I'm just saying, you've got to be in this heart space. The guru does not tell you that, be it man or woman, because you have to find this out for yourself. It has to be a free choice. I'm not promoting gurus here; I'm simply saying that this is the resolution.

The ELF waves stimulate that device, along with other things. The government puts out ELF rays to generate passivity or aggression?

Yes, but interestingly enough, some of the people down a ways in the pecking order know that when they broadcast the ELF waves it seems to have effects on you, and that's all they know. There is no need for them to know.

Oh, what they're doing.

Yes, there is no need for them to know about this dormant seed. So this is not widely known, needless to say, in the rank and file. It's like in the military; you know only what you need to know.

Beginnings of the Secret Government

Now, let's come forward. Who became the controllers of the planet on the Earth's surface, and when, in our historical time?

Remember, people are *born* to this role, one generation after another.

But where did it start?

It really started sequencing one generation after another about 80,000 years ago.

Talk a little bit about that.

This occurred when Orion people realized they needed to get seawater and might need to see through the eyes of a human being. Their devices to see the future can get a broad perspective that they cannot usually get without going through a lot of struggle and doing dangerous things. They usually get the perspective from a person's future or their succeeding generations by taking a person on board their ship. They already know that generally somewhere in the future of this person one descendant will become influential. They attach a device that looks similar to a backpack, something that fits over your shoulders and has radiating bits and pieces down your back (not below the base of your spine, though, just above the curvature of your lower spine). There are a couple of probes that come around and attach about an inch and a half or two inches below your temporal mandibula.

That's how you described that inculcating device, so it works both ways.

That's right. The device attaches to the side of your neck, and then oftentimes it will have several different parts that attach to the top of the skull.

It looks like acupuncture needles, you said.

Yes. You can sit or stand, whichever is comfortable; it takes only a moment. They stand behind you, they have a scope back there, a readout device, that can scan succeeding generations. If something happens to succeeding generations and your line does not go forward, then it just goes black. The family has died out at that point. But if they think you are going to be the great-great-grandfather of a future premier, they look forward and see what that person is going to be like, sort of a negotiating point. Then they unstrap you and sit down, take you around the ship, walk around — they're not unfriendly. Look at this, look at that, have something to eat, whatever. It's sociable. Then with an attachment device not much bigger than your forefinger they reach around the back of your head and touch you lightly on the right side of your head at the temple. You forget everything and go into sort of a relaxed state like a deep meditative state. You might fall down, so they have someone near you to catch you. Then they take you back to where they found you. You don't remember anything, though you might remember it in dreams. Or it might come back in bits and pieces to a person who is bound and determined to figure out where they've been for the last three days.

And then reversed, they can feed information into you very quickly?

Yes, the other way. It's a useful device, but of course it's basically a device that is not good for practice.

So 80,000 years ago they started looking into the future? They starting seeing they needed seawater . . .

By that time they knew they needed seawater, and from time to time they'd need a little sand — you know, quartz. They didn't take crystals. They needed polarized crystals, so they'd take white sand. That suited their purpose fine, and it was available here. They didn't need much, and they'd take it from places where it would go unnoticed, which would be even better. Very often they'd go into the sea and do it; then they could load up a ship, take maybe a hundred thousand gallons of seawater that would last them maybe 5000 years. But they didn't usually do that. They would take maybe 100 gallons here, 1000 gallons there because they could come and go at will. That gave them the excuse to come here, and everybody wanted to come here. So that's what they would do, and it became a regular thing.

That's really how it started. At that point, they realized they would be coming here all the time. They knew that at some point they would be detected and there would be a problem. So they needed to be influential; they needed to have friends in high places, as it were. So they started talking to the people living in the under- ground bases. At that time, there were still lots of people living on the surface. They told the people in the underground base, "We need to start having you go up to the surface." When people heard that underneath the planet, they said, "Oh, no, no, we don't want to do that, it's hostile up there."

The Orions said, "Look, we need to have a group of you. We're not going to draft anybody. We want volunteers who feel a little more adventurous. We'll help you, we'll support you. You will achieve levels of power in the society and be the leaders of today, tomorrow and the future. It's a big responsibility. You will be able to return home to the underground bases from time to time, and people will also come out from here and visit with you. Eventually, when you feel safe, you can bring your families. You might even find that you enjoy some of the people on the surface." The people couldn't imagine that, but the Orions were trying to plant the seed thought that the Atlanteans would eventually commingle with the people on the surface. Eventually they had a small cadre of about a hundred people that volunteered.

Are these from that big South African underground base?

These are from both Iceland and South Africa. Not too many, but all young people, for the most part, who'd be looking for something adventurous, something fun to do, something different, and who'd like the idea of being able to direct things. From their point of view, that cadre of people would be thinking, generally, "Well, here we have a perfect balanced society. Everything is working fine for us down here. Maybe we can help the people on the surface if we can exert some level of control over their society. If we run things, then things will be all right." That was their attitude in the beginning. So they came to the surface and established themselves. It took them about 2000 years of their generation and succeeding generations, and lo and behold, they gradually began intermarrying with surface peoples, liking them, educating them, as it were, and bringing some into the fold, from their point of view.

In the process, they also planted the seed of their own spiritual evolution. They did this and succeeding generations were born to the task. They checked, you know, as the babies were born. Is it this one, has he got the dedication? Is it this one, has she got the loyalty? Eventually they figured out which babies were the right ones, and they passed that skill on to succeeding generations. Before long, they had a small group of influential people who were in a position, with the help of the ETs, to be able to be sufficiently influential to keep things going.

At first they took positions at the head of the government, thinking that was the way to do it. Then they realized, no, no, that's totally off, because they were constantly being barraged by other issues they had no interest but which the people they were leading cared about. They said, this is not good at all. After a few hundred years of that error, they realized that *they* didn't need to be visible; they needed to be behind the scenes. They needed to be wealthy, they needed to be influential, but all behind the scenes. And not a wealth that is obvious. But they needed to have money or whatever the medium of exchange was, some means of visiting power on whoever was the head of the government so that those people would want to please them. That's what they concentrated on doing; that's essentially what they are doing to this day.

Perversion of Their Original Intention

One more thing: Let's remember their original purpose. That was to create a society, albeit somewhat controlled, that would not have any wars or violence, that could sustain itself, where everyone had a job they were born to, and there would always be enough for everyone. Of course, this is a very controlled society. You have to remember that this is their original motivation. But they also had to deal with the polarities of the planet, what people liked. They had to provide them what they like so they can remain an influence, and sometimes they have to deal with the fact that ETs may be behind their back and they don't even know it. Not all ETs, just some of the negative Orion warriors who are stirring up the pot, getting people fascinated with the idea of drugs and other corruptions. Eventually they find themselves in the uncomfortable position — and believe me, they're very uncomfortable — of having to provide drugs or the means to drugs or the means to wealth or the means of corruption to the people in power so that they will be able to run things from behind the scenes. Thus they find themselves actually providing the *opposite* of what their original intention was.

I can't tell you how many times they have said, "If we can only get through this time and get past this, the people will realize the error of their ways and see that drugs are destructive in all forms. But they say, "If we can only get through this time, then we can help them to create a controlled, benevolent society." That's their point of view.

But always controlled.

Always controlled so that the people's tendency toward any violence, which they see as a factor, will be controlled — not controlled rigidly, authoritarianlike, but channeled into something constructive.

Like wars.

Well, from their point of view, they don't like wars. They don't want wars. We're talking about the Atlantean descendants here, we're not talking about the negative ETs. They would like to see people channel their destructive or violent energy into sport. They like sport — football, rugby, things that can be essentially aggressive and violent.

. . . and organized.

Yes, organized and controlled. Nevertheless, they see sport as the saving grace, the thing that they can do. So they're spreading sport all over the planet like crazy, hoping this will give people an outlet. They're not in the dark anymore, they're not foolish anymore. They've had Earth experience, and know that these ETs they made a deal with a long time ago are not doing them a lot of good. But they can't do anything about it. It's a deal they can't get out of; it's in their genetic code. They're stuck with it.

ET Intentions

So what else do these ETs want? They want much more than a little sand and a little seawater now, in 1994.

Some of them want absolute authority to mine the Moon.

Well, but that's also some other friends. Some of the Orions want that, too.

Yes, some of them want absolute authority to mine the Earth. And our Atlantean descendant friends that may be corrupted —yes, not of their own choosing, but there they are, living in it. It's like they're standing in the mud and wishing they weren't. But they are, and they had to become what they've seen others become. It's very ironic. They are confronted even to this day with these beings who have superior technology who want to mine the Earth and *are* mining the Earth under the sea right now, where they are somewhat detectable. But no one can really do anything about it. And here they're mining the Earth, taking things, digging around in Earth. Part of the reason Earth is going through these many changes is because they're digging in deep, real deep. You know, human beings are digging around the surface, but these guys are down 800-900 miles digging.

Under the ocean.

Yes. 800-900 miles inward. That's dangerous. That's creating real problems for Mother Earth. So she has to get rid of it. She can do it, but not without causing major harm to everyone, including herself. It is an odd thing, but a good thing you're shifting dimensions, because that will change it.

Okay, how many of these shadow-government Atlantean descendants are now on the planet in a position of power?

Rather in a position of influence, I'd say. Right now, a shockingly small number. I'm going to include their personal aides, who are least somewhat in the know; I'm going to include their personal families, who are also somewhat in the know, and give you a number of about 1800. If I give you the exact number, it wouldn't be that hard to detect them.

Why?

I can't tell you any more. If you detected them, and if you found them, it would change the motivational energies of what you are going through now. That is not good. Interestingly enough, I find myself in the awkward position of having to protect them!

So the people that are in the news, like the Rockefellers and the German bankers and Kissingers and all that, they're not them?

No.

They're the front line.

If you see them, they are not them. Never forget that. That's the key. If you see the people, if you know their names, you know for *certain* they are not these people.

So then all the stuff that's publicized about the Trilaterals and the Council of Foreign Relations, that's not the guys behind the scenes, then?

No. If they are visible, they are not the shadow government.

But these visible ones, then, out there making these decisions and having these meetings and passing these orders are acting on the orders of the shadow government.

Yes, but usually not directly, usually indirectly. If any desire goes directly from a member of the shadow government to somebody who is actively functioning in society in a visible position, that shadow government person is seriously compromised in their security. It goes through many, many channels before it gets to the person who's actually exposed, say a person sitting on the Trilateral Commission, whose names you can get. That's an exposed person.

But they know when it comes from . . .

They have their own motivations, and the reason they're on the Commission in the first place is they believe in what the Commission is doing. They may be influenced by other parties who, from their point of view, are a perfectly worthwhile influence, and sometimes by regular citizens and sometimes by people on the chain, as it were. Sometimes they get influencing dreams. You can't get rid of that.

Well then, how does this shadow government control everything? You said they ran the planet from this base underneath the Cape of Good Hope.

How the Basic Control Works; Negative Sirians

I can't tell you the exact way. If I tell you the exact way, you can stop it. Do you know what happens if you stop it? You stop your shift in dimension, too. The only reason you're shifting from the third to the fourth dimension is to get away from this. You're in mid-shift.

Satisfy my curiosity without doing anything detrimental to our plans here, okay?

I will say they are able to do it through radionics that affect genetics.

Okay, I understand. The negative Sirians – where do they figure in this?

The negative Sirians know that Earth is associated with them somehow. They're coming from a position where they feel the Earth is their territory and they want it back. They feel that Earth people are competing for their space and they want it. So they are the eight ball in the situation. They cannot be trusted, so they're like the Orions, or those from Xpotaz or other sources; they are sort of like a pest. So the shadow government and the allies find themselves in the curious position of having to protect your planet from the negative Sirians because these people are pests, from their point of view. That's another function of Star Wars.

How are they being pesky? They say they have this incredible weapon nobody thinks they have?

The secret government is reasonably certain that the incredible weapon is nonexistent. They have heard this from the Orions, but they do not trust the Orions, and that's probably appropriate. However, in this case I feel that the secret weapon is not a real weapon but a device that can eliminate planets, yes, but only works under certain very specific conditions. It is essentially a programmed weapon that can only be used for defensive purposes. It cannot be used for offensive purposes. So in that sense it works, but it can't . . .

But if they don't have a planet to defend?

That's right. They think they do, but since in fact they don't, then it won't work. But more importantly, it *hasn't* worked! What does that suggest to you? They tried it, and it hasn't worked. But they know it works because they've used it in defensive situations before. It doesn't work now and they cannot understand it, because they feel personally threatened.

Yes, because they believe this is their planet. And since we borrowed it from the Sirians, they might be sort of right, huh?

They are right. But they're using their knowledge in their own way. That is to be expected, because they are unsophisticated.

Okay, but what are they doing on the planet?

They are trying to come down and influence people. They've built their own underground bases.

Which one? Dulce?

All right. They're trying to influence people, but most of their experiments go awry. Since the minute the people that they could create or influence go to the surface of the planet, they are immediately bombarded with what's going on (even under the surface they're somewhat bombarded, but they are a little more insulated) — and then they're transformed.

So they're not having any luck. The shadow government just has to tolerate them, but its ultimate intention is to get rid of them. But they really don't have anything to worry about, and cooler heads in the shadow government prevail. Occasionally hotheads flare up and they just say, let's just blast them out of the sky, but cooler heads understand that it's better to let a small outpost be here and have no success than to react and send many, many ships. They would then find out that they're in a battle and it's ongoing. So cooler heads are performing their tasks.

The Xpotaz, the Orions and the Grays

So all this stuff that I asked you the other day about these few people that came in from 1890 are really almost irrelevant.

Not irrelevant. It's all relevant, but it's in layers, within context.

What about the Xpotaz who gave them the flying machine that travels in time?

That really flew in the face of what Orions were attempting to do, because they wanted to be ultimately authoritarian. Now they find, much to their shock, that this group of renegades who, they hoped, would be totally and ultimately their ally, was now sort of like a second-cousin ally. It's like the Xpotaz don't really need them anymore, and they don't like that. It's created a tremendous amount of friction between the space pirates (as we're calling those from Xpotaz for the sake of our story) and the Orions, but we have a situation where people are tolerating each other. It is like, okay, pirates, we have to put up with you, so we will; you're not worth the bother right now.

How do we put all of this into something that makes sense? The shadow government got that little flying disk engine from the Zetas (then the Grays); is that also in use right now?

Let's not call the Grays and the Zetas the same people. The Grays are a less sophisticated version of the Zetas.

Do they have a name?

Let's see if we can come up with a name in their language. From the Zetas' point of view, they'd be the students.

When did the shadow government . . .

Understand this to begin with: None of the dates can match because of where you are in your cycle of time right now. Dates are absolutely arbitrary.

I'm only talking about the last hundred years.

Even those are arbitrary.

Okay, the Xpotaz came in 1890 and they were towing the ship, but you told me that the ship didn't come till 1930.

I cannot make it like that for you. Write in your own dates, it's really like that. If your time was once linear, now your time is cycling like this, dates are literally meaningless.

If we say 1890, the Xpotaz brought that ship with them when they came then. That big, two-and-a-half-mile manufacturing ship.

All right.

They did?

Yes.

Okay, did they have any other ships like it?

Like that? No. But they had smaller ships.

The Orions are not in league with the Renegades [those from Xpotaz], and the Renegades do not see the Orions as much of a threat. They look at the Orions as people who simply are miners and engineers. There was not really what I call a brotherly relationship between these people, but there was a level of tolerance. The Renegades would have been the ones who had fleshed out the base a little bit more with equipment and so on for the shadow government. Not the Orions; the Orions had no need to do that. However, in the process of fleshing out the base, the Renegades made it less easy for the Orions to use the base. The Orions would have to come into the area where they had screened off the section that I mentioned. The Orions would not be as socially welcome in other parts of the base that were socially impacted by the Renegades. So it created kind of a competition. In some cases, it was a good-natured competition, but in most cases it was just a discomfort. Almost like people nowadays have discomfort with people from other nationalities, and mostly it's a mistrust based on ignorance. That's what you had there.

The whole thing didn't really take off until the 1890s when the Xpotaz came, and that's when the real coming together of the shadow government occurred, when things really started to focus, right?

From your frame of reference, yes. Things really started to focus about 80,000 years ago, but obviously that had nothing to do with your modern times, or only indirectly. From the point of view of what originally started this entire conversation about the recent disk crash, from 1890 forward in your old time (T-1), would be the most important factor. Of course, now you're in T-3, but that's another story.

Can we put some of these things that are in the literature now in perspective? Who was in the crash of 1947 at Roswell? What was that about?

To my understanding, as I see the people, I see them as a version of the Zeta beings.

Did they come from Dulce? Were they manufactured to exist on the surface from Dulce?

I don't think the beings originated from any Earthbound location. As near as I can tell, they originated from a small planet near, but not within, the Zeta Reticulum system.

But not what we call the Grays?

I don't believe that these people are what would be referred to from the Zeta perspective as the students, referred to now as the Grays, but it's not a term I like. I feel that these people were different.

What were they doing here? How did they get shot down?

It was not really *shot* down. At that time that base in Roswell was perhaps the only base where long-range radar was being experimented with. Today that would not be particularly secret to the services. In those days, they had radar on the ground. They wanted it in the sky, but they knew they had to get the bandwidth figured out first. So what they would do is make more and more powerful radar. What they didn't understand is that the radiation went not just where the antenna directed it, but it created a radiating field in all directions. (I might say that some of the people on this base, not all, got sick in later life as a result, which was certainly not the intention of the people who were experimenting with the radar.) But this ship, which was flying close to the ground, albeit not visibly, went through this incredibly powerful field and it totally disrupted their vehicle's ability to maneuver. You have to understand that the disks essentially fly on magnetic fields. They move by their own power, but what keeps them suspended, from falling like a stone, is the magnetic field of the Earth. So this radar experiment was disrupting the magnetic field of the Earth in that area. Because the disruption occurred so long and so far, the ship tried valiantly to stay airborne, but it could not. As they pumped more into power and to keeping airborne, it became visible and eventually crashed.

Why were they here?

They were here as part of the observational staff. They were not directly in contact with human beings as were the students of the Zeta beings who *are* more directly involved. They were essentially in training — trainees, if you will.

Essentially sightseeing.

Sightseeing in a sense, but also keeping an eye on military bases. You have to remember that this base at that time was also associated with the atomic devices, so they were trying to keep an eye on it. They did not understand the problem with the radar. That's to be expected, since they were not as sophisticated as the people who were teaching them. It was an unfortunate accident.

In 1947 what was Kenneth Arnold watching? Whose were those craft that he was seeing?

Are we talking about the disk that was skipping along whereby people suddenly started calling them flying saucers?

Yes.

They were not doing so much. They were coming from an underground base that had been established many, many years ago, and they had emerged from the base. When he saw them, they were apparently coming from this mountain where they had emerged on the other side, and had not yet done anything to mask themselves. He saw them and was able to keep up with them for a short period of time, until they eventually masked themselves. But at that time, in the '40s, it was still relatively innocent. The ships would appear; there would not be any reason to mask them, since there was not any direct threat to them, they thought, not understanding the effect of radar, which they only understood later.

Who were these guys?

These people were Andromedans.

And the base was on the other side? In the Rockies?

In the Rockies, let's say.

All right. In all of our literature this starts in the '40s, but that's ridiculous. That's only the first time we saw them.

Well, if you really research, you can trace this back to the 1890s, but a lot of documents have been lost over the years.

The excitement on this planet mostly goes back to the '40s.

Yes, yes, that's really true. It sort of began in World War II with the idea of foo fighters.

The Fawns: Part Zeta, Part Human

The 1954 Edwards Air Force Base meeting supposedly with Eisenhower —

who did he meet with?

I believe he met with a form of the Zeta beings that I have referred to before as being a cross between Zetas and humans. These people would have a little more emotion, they would look very definitely extraterrestrial, but they would not be so obscurely different that one would feel . . .

Are we talking about what we call the half-breed?

I don't like that term.

The Essassani?

I don't want to say they're the Essassani, because they are from a specific place. We're talking about people who have been referred to before as the Fawn group. These people are about 51% Zeta and 49% human, so they have a lot of human emotions, feelings, passions.

Where do they live? I've never come across this word before. Where is their planet?

Their planet is within the Zeta Reticulum system.

Why were they here? What did they want? Were they emissaries of somebody else?

That's true. Someone asked them to come here to make contact, to be on board the ship. There were other people on the ship, but someone asked them. They were not here only by themselves. If you read the literature closely, there was more than one ship. One of the ships was the Renegades'. The Fawn ship was essentially here to keep peace so that the Renegades wouldn't do anything crazy, from the Zeta's perspective. They wouldn't say, "Oh, we'll show you how powerful we are," and blow up a barracks with a hundred people in it. So the Fawn group kept things light and fun: "Let's show them, let's go down the air strip with the disk on the side, and do things that can't be done." They kept it light.

Who asked the Fawn ship to come? The Zetas?

Yes. Not the Renegades. The Renegades took their appearance in stride and clearly recognized that the Fawns were here to try and keep peace.

The Renegades

Why were the Renegades there?

To create an alliance with the then-surface government of this country, in which they had lots of bases. They were beginning to be detected and were having to move their bases deeper. Radar penetrates underground, but not very well. It can't be read clearly, but they did not know that. The Renegades thought that the radar signal was actually detecting their presence and the people on the surface knew they were there. Imagine their surprise when they found out it wasn't! Here they showed up, made this whole big display of themselves and were talking to these people thinking that Eisenhower already knew about them. Imagine their surprise when they discovered they had revealed themselves unnecessarily.

Okay, but why to Eisenhower? He was just the president of one country. Why not to the shadow government?

Eisenhower had been the supreme commander in World War II. He knew all about foo fighters. Eisenhower was a man with many secrets, being a general as he was and with the tremendous responsibility he had. They perceived Eisenhower to be the most powerful and influential surface dweller of the time.

But why would the Renegades go around the secret government?

In other cases they might have gone to General Montgomery or General DeGaulle. But the point of fact is that World War II was a world-involved war and Eisenhower was in command. So they came to him.

We're saying the shadow government controlled the planet, and yet here we have these Renegades coming to Eisenhower because they thought he was the most powerful being on the planet. Didn't they have any sense that since they had an alliance with the shadow government, they were doing something that was out of bounds?

Certainly they did. They were fully in realization that they were going to have trouble with the shadow government, because at that point the shadow government was more powerful than they had expected. After all, the shadow government had alliances with *others*.

So there's no Orions in here.

No, there's no Orions in this picture, but the Renegades knew the shadow government was operating with somebody else and they recognized that they needed to have an ally, too. They wanted to reach out and ally themselves with governments of the world, especially reaching to a man who had just gone through this terrible war where he had directed the successful victory. They figured if anybody would understand allies, if anybody would appreciate the value of what they had to offer, this man was that person. However, they did not count on Eisenhower's highly moral values. Eisenhower was a very moral person. Even though he had to go along with certain things, it was uncomfortable. Others around him were willing to go along with these things more easily.

What did he have to go along with?

He had to accept the fact that there were beings on Earth, within Earth, who had power over human beings, and he did not like that. After all, he had dedicated his life to freeing human beings to pursue happiness freely, as it says in the Constitution, and here he's faced with people who have influence on and manipulate human beings, and there's nothing he can do about it. As a military man he knows from their weapons display, by the simple act of the ships flying around everywhere, that there's nothing we can do about it. He feels terribly helpless. Can you imagine how he feels, after his victory over the Nazis ? Very frustrated. I might add that this eventually contributed to his death. He realized that he was being placed in an untenable position. It was his nature to rescue people and help them to live a better life, or to put them in the least amount of risk possible. Ask any of the people who served under him, the GIs, or the French forces, for that matter. He would never put people at risk when it could be avoided. He would take chances that were absolutely necessary, but he always protected the troops to the best of his ability. But here he was, the leader of the United States at that time, with his people in danger and there was nothing he could do about it. He couldn't even *tell* the people about it. Can you imagine his frustration?

And yet Truman knew about the flying saucers during the Second World War. Is that not right? Was Truman allied with the shadow government?

No. Again, this is a very moral man.

But he knew about it.

He knew about it, but there wasn't much he could do about it. Someone says, "We're flying along and this thing appears next to us and they're observing us. I'm in this major battle," a pilot might be saying, "fighting for my life, and this silly disk is flying around me, and there's nothing I can do about it. What can we do about it, Mr. President?" Of course, this isn't directed to the President, but it's through channels. He couldn't do anything about it.

Majestic Twelve

Who started this highly touted, this Majestic Twelve? Did Eisenhower start it? Did the shadow government start it?

I'm going to say a name that you've always loved, and I'm going to apologize to this person's relatives and say to you outright that it is not my intention to throw mud on this man. For this man did not fully grasp that he was aligned with anything corrupting. He thought he was doing the right thing, but there were influences. I want this in print: There were influences upon him and he did not understand who these people were. This man —John Foster Dulles —did not realize who he was involved with.

But he thought he was protecting the sanity of the planet.

He thought he was protecting the *sanctity of the free world!* He did not realize that he was being manipulated, and this is not a man who was easily manipulated. He did not realize that he was being manipulated by agents of the shadow government.

Once that started, that's when the secrecy lid went on, the ridicule, everything.

That's right. The tactic, which, as everyone knows today, was a big mistake. But you could look at the times and ask, well, what else might they have done? They did not realize the policy would live on long past the point of where it is now. It is totally ludicrous. They figured they would keep it secret for about ten years, and then let it out slowly.

Then what happened?

By that time those people were no longer in power. When they wanted to talk about it, they were told that, no, it will be revealed later. Of course, a lot of these people died off.

The policy was just perpetuated?

It was perpetuated, yes, by people who said, "Well, how can we tell them *now?* We'll look like fools." Most importantly, from their point of view, "How can we tell Earth people about this *and* tell them that there's nothing we can do about it?" That's their real position.

Somebody said, what better way to cover up your weapons than to have people ridicule the subject?

It's a good way, but it doesn't last. As anybody knows who's gone through high school, someone might ridicule you for a while, but at some point you learn how to take it in stride, you laugh about it, maybe you have a fight with someone and the ridicule is over. At some point it is resolved. This policy is laughable today, that UFOs don't exist.

Is the shadow government perpetuating it?

No, they think it's funny, too.

So it's just bureaucratically going on, then?

I don't want to call it bureaucratic. It recently came out that the government has known for forty-odd years that all this is real. People are going to say, "What do we need *you* for? How can we trust you?" As it is, because of many other policies, they're saying that anyway. Probably future presidents are going to inherit the wrath, even though it was done by earlier people. Let's not blame anybody. This was all done by people who were manipulated. Let's never forget that.

But they killed a lot of people in the '50s. This was not just a light policy, they killed anybody who tried to put the truth out.

Isn't it odd? Everybody was trying to promote their point of view, and sometimes when you try to do that you lose sight of your values and pretty soon everybody's using the same tactics — the police and the policed or criminals — because everybody believes they're right. Things descend to that level.

So exactly when did the shadow government get the functional flying disk with the optical-illusion technology? Was it from the Xpotaz time machine or from the Grays?

The first one they had was really vehicles that were shot down. They were able to pull off pieces and figure out roughly how it worked. But they didn't get a working model visited upon them by the Renegades until about the '60s.

Renegade Time Travel and Protective Device

Could the Renegades time-travel then, or was it 1991?

From their point of view, suppose a ship goes back in time and can't get back? They were not too concerned about the crew, to be perfectly honest, but what happens to the ship? Their point of view was, let's not do this until we're absolutely certain that we can get it back. However, who's experimenting in time travel? Montauk. Let's wait and see if *they* have some success.

They waited. Montauk didn't have any success, not absolutely guaranteed. The success they had always had risk factors. So they gave up on Montauk because of the instability of people's dark sides and how to dominate them. They went back to negotiating for a ship. It was really not until the late '80s, after many experiments, that they started going back in time with the ship — and, I might add, holding their breath — sending it back for only a microsecond, disappearing in the present and coming back in the same second. Really being very cautious.

So that's why they didn't disappear the President until 1991; that's the first time they actually had the technology to do it.

That's the first time they used the technology they had and took a chance, from their point of view. They said, "Well, maybe the ship won't come back, but we have to try."

You said the Cape of Good Hope, the international headquarters of the secret government, has this weapon that can disrupt anything within 300 miles. I realize this is an incredible protective device. Did the Orions know that when they put the base there, or did they learn that later? No one could ever get close to them if they had this weapon. They are totally secure forever.

The weapon wasn't there initially. You're talking about something way back.

Could the Orions see that far into the future? Did they know that this would be the ultimate place . . . ?

No, when they saw into the future they would get a broad view of what was happening, but they could not get infinitesimal details unless they used the device that looked through people's eyes at future generations. The more people they have, the more unlikely that's going to work.

So that was just a fortuitous coincidence, then.

No coincidence, but the fact of the matter is that they did not see that weapon system coming.

So whose technology, the Renegades'?

Yes.

They saw the potential for it.

They saw the potential, the advantage. They saw that it could give them an edge over the negative Orions, whom they did not actually worry about too much.

But they are totally secure there.

Yes, they are totally secure. Nobody can approach them in any vehicle, rather no *organic* entity can approach them. They can be approached only by an interdimensional entity that remains interdimensional. In a sense, an advanced benevolent Orion ship of today traveling in Light, maintaining, say, a ninth-dimensional vibration, can travel right into their base and be there, but cannot become physical and *do* anything. They have to remain at the ninth dimension and fly out. When something becomes physical, it can be disrupted. That's how they're able to do what they wish to do. But it's also, for that matter, how others know exactly what the Renegades are doing. You can go there as a ninth-dimensional being and walk around their base, watching them and reporting exactly what they're doing. But you could not actually affect it except through spiritual means.

The Sedona Area Activity

The secret government's flying disks that are now headquartered in Secret Canyon: The nautical miles they are moving are straight up into a space station, correct?

I can't say without creating total *threat for them.* They are moving from here to a place within plain sight where they can't be detected. I cannot contribute to a threat for anybody else, no matter whether the people are totally awful or wonderful.

Where do they get their pilots for these flying disks? They must take the top guns from the Air Force Academy?

No, they do not do that; those people would be missed. They tend to recruit people who may have washed out of the Air Force Academy (but not anybody of recent generation, so don't worry; I'm not singling anybody out). They take people who are not that great as pilots and give them their advanced training techniques, to say nothing of the inculcation that packs knowledge and information beyond their mental capacity sometimes. This has the effect of either breaking down the brain so the IQ is lowered, but at other times has the effect of raising the IQ. They hope that it raises the IQ. If it does, they use those people; if it doesn't, they don't use them. They tend to recruit from the more obscure places people who already have the desire to fly or people who are already flying something or have had the pleasure of flying. They don't want to recruit anybody who would be absolutely missed. They also try not to recruit anybody with living blood relatives. They'd prefer to recruit orphans, and ideally orphans that are not married and do not have girlfriends or boyfriends who'd miss them.

So you'd never get through with it, then. You'd never get out. There's no way you could wipe a brain that's been inculcated, right?

No, once you've been inculcated, it's there. But you do have the opportunity to retire. They don't just take them out in a field and put a bullet in their brain, as it were. It's not to a benevolent Earth life; you don't go to a farm and work with cattle.

Where would you go, to the back of the Moon or someplace?

You might go to the other side of the Moon. You might retire to the underground base in a benevolent surrounding of some sort. But it would not likely be the surface of the Earth. You might be able to go on vacation to the surface of the Earth in various places with others, but your freedom is compromised from the time you agree to join them. Once you're with these people, your freedom is compromised.

What is the shape of the flying saucer? Can you draw it?

I can say it: It's triangular.

It looks like a delta wing?

It's more triangular than that. If you take the shape of the Great Pyramid of Gizeh and stretch it out a little bit, it's like that. It's not like a Stealth bomber or anything like that. It looks like a thick triangle.

So it's not in any way saucer-shaped?

No. They do have a couple of disks, and we refer to them as disks, but — I'm actually stretching it, by telling you a triangular shape.

But there are other triangular shapes out there. The Xpotaz must have triangular shapes if that's where the government got them from.

Not necessarily. It's a great way to keep track of your own ships versus the ships you're giving to somebody. "If it's a triangle, it's not one of us." It's a basic tactic.

So they didn't actually give them one of their own ships. They actually told them how to make one.

They would give them ships, and the triangular ones would be their ships. But they wouldn't be as powerful, as strong, as flexible and, most important, they wouldn't *look* exactly like one of their ships. That way even if you couldn't tell by any means if both ships were physically there, your could say, "Well, that's a disk, so that's ours; that's a triangle, so that's theirs." Very simple. Also you would know that practically no other extraterrestrials visiting this planet have triangular ships. There wouldn't be much risk of accidentally shooting down one of somebody else's ships and then having to find yourself in a fight with them or being in a ticklish position. You want to give people a ship that is odd-looking.

To get back to the moment: We've got reports of jets strafing, of jets and flying disks crashing into rocks, when that's really an optical illusion — they're going right through them. There's a lot of helicopters, a lot of action going on here. What's going on?

Most of the basic military forces of the United States and any other place do not know about these alliances. Or if they know about them, they cannot accept it. You could read it in a magazine and say, "That's one thing, but until my general tells me, I don't believe it." That's a reasonable position for any military person. If you're going to see something flying around where you think it oughtn't to be and you warn them not to fly there, from a military position you might be inclined to ask permission to shoot at this thing, especially if you think it is a threat.

Their superiors don't necessarily know about this . . .

Sometimes they might know; sometimes it might be jets that are under the influence of the shadow government. Most of the time they are not, because that government's entire point of view is to remain invisible. So they are not going to have too many surface forces; they might sneak a jet up there at some point, but not often.

So these strafing runs that are being seen are regular U.S. military chasing after something they think shouldn't be there.

Exactly. Sometimes when these things fly into a cliff, there might be a blast of light behind them that would look startlingly like an explosion. Sometimes when people go there and find bits and pieces, those bits and pieces have been left there to leave the illusion that the ship was shot down. Most of the time it isn't. But it's a great way to cover your backside, as it were. The submarines during war sometimes threw a little oil, a little wreckage up on the surface so the enemy would think they were dead.

The Transformation of the Shadow Government

The shadow government knows we're going into another dimension and they want to stop it because they can't control it.

They'd love to slow it down. They know they can't stop it, though they'd like to. They'd like to slow it down so they can figure out where they are and what they can do, and then assess their position militarily. They're having a slight effect like you'd have if you were driving along in a car and you hung your foot out the door. It's not much; it could be measured by a good physicist.

You said these are the ones, the controllers, who are going to be purified, the very Atlanteans who have been doing this so nobly for so long, from your point of view?

Let's take them back to where they started in Lemuria. They have to reexperience their memories so they can see how they got to be where they are. From one point of view, these are their ancestors. They have to arrive at a certain future point, do something that is totally the antithesis of their original intent, and be totally in the feeling of that. That's the most important thing, being in the feeling of it, the emotion of it. When they are emotionally participating in something that is the *antithesis*, the opposite, of what they originally wanted to do, then we take them back. They still have all those feelings when they arrive back at the point they started, and they say, "My, god, how could this have happened?" Then they *willingly* wish to be transformed. This can only be done with their approval. It has to be done at the exact moment so they can understand how they got from A to B, as it were. When they understand that, then they will see that *if they just make a different choice* it will be better.

They're playing the same role as Lucifer. They are accelerating us into the fourth dimension.

They're pushing you. You're being pulled, and they are, inadvertently, pushing you. Much as they would like to be holding you back, they are pushing you!

Yet when you look at Lucifer and the whole planetary situation, we had to do all this to get into the third dimension to touch this deep density, to do what we came to do.

Yes, to resolve not only how to create planets, how to be Creators, but also to understand your full responsibility to all life and the consequences of all your actions. One might, as a Creator, get angry and think "I should do this" and catch yourself and say, "No, no, I'm the Creator, I can't do that." *You can't afford to do that.* In that brief moment of "I should do this" you've already done it and can't put it back. At the Creator level you really can't afford to make mistakes. So you get to come here and make *all kinds* of mistakes and get it out of your system.

And we've done that. Were you on that first planet that blew up in this space where the 50-foot beings were?

I can't put anything over on you, can I? You'd get it eventually. I was, and that's why I'm *here*.

How long do you have to hang around? You and Lucifer and Jehovah . . .

. . . To say nothing of many others. We'll hang in there till the planet gets back to Sirius. We'll also be active in both places. Then we'll probably stay with you until you get to about the sixth or seventh dimension in your souls' journey into your ultimate experience — when you're at the point where you start replacing the Creator on His coffee break. And then we will . . .

And you get to be free!

. . . tip our etheric hats to you and go our own way, thank you!

But if we get to be Creators, what do you get to be?

We'll go with the Creator that's there now. We'll go to the next level. So we also are motivated.

Let's move this ship!

So *much* is going on. It is really odd to be physically alive during these times. Normally a planet goes through this when the animals are no longer there. So the animals are really looking forward to all of you "getting it" real soon, because they'd like to be elsewhere as soon as they can.

All this time you've been talking about the negative Sirians inheriting this planet. That's going to be when it gets back to Sirius?

Yes. Things have changed. It's actually much better for them to stay in their own solar system. They're going to move on the soul level to Earth as a Sirius planet. They will again be somewhat isolated and polarized somewhat from their version — half positive, half negative. This 50% will be a radical change for them — and they'll go through a cycle not unlike what you've been through here. Eventually they'll be welcomed back into the fold of all benevolent beings. But they must go through that cycle, so they will have to be in a remote and isolated spot.

Where are we going? There was to be a fourth-dimensional Terra here in the solar system.

Right now as we speak there are other levels of Earth. There are other levels of Terra, which was the planet that was here before. So on the soul level many of you will go all over the place. Those of you who stay in the general area will be ensouled, embodied on probably the upper dimensions of Terra.

Which won't be a beautiful ocean planet like this one.

No, but it will be pretty nice.

UFO Researcher Witnesses Battle in the Sky

by Tom Dongo
August 26, 1994

Before I go into the UFO incident that is the point of this article, I want to mention that at the time of this writing, August 26, 1994, I have experienced four UFO sightings in twenty-one days. However, this most recent experience was, to put it mildly, more dramatic than the first three. The first and second occurred as I was giving an outdoor UFO talk to fifteen people; a UFO flew toward us. As it got closer it simply blinked out. There was a similar sighting later on in the evening. The third sighting took place as Sedona resident Dr. Carlos Warter was hypnotically regressing a Sedona resident who had recently been abducted. I watched from outside on Dr. Warter's back deck as a ball of white light, which I thought at first was an airplane's landing lights, exploded into a far larger light. For several seconds the expanded light from this object actually bent upward as it turned and then streaked off into space.

In discussing the fourth sighting, I will mention, for credibility purposes, that two other adult witnesses four miles from where I was saw the same things I did but from an entirely different vantage point. On the day of this incident, August 23, I had been feeling low on energy and tremendously out of sorts. I just couldn't get up to speed all day. I had been invited to go on a hike at 6:00 p.m. with a group of friends. I opted not to go, which is very unlike me. Instead,

I decided to sleep in my van out in the canyons that night and went out early to a favorite campsite. If I had not declined the hike, I would not have had the experience that night.

It got dark about 7:45 p.m. and as it grew darker I noticed that more jet aircraft than usual were flying around in the night sky. A major east/west air route crosses over Sedona, so commercial jet traffic here is common. I noticed that night, though, that some of these high-flying jets were nowhere near the usual commercial air corridors. As the minutes passed and it got progressively darker. (There was an almost-full moon that night, but it didn't rise until 9:00 p.m.) I couldn't help noticing that jets were becoming more and more numerous. Then formations of jet fighters began showing up and were criss-crossing the cloudless, completely clear night sky in differing directions and at differing altitudes. There were jets in ones, twos, threes and fives flying within sight of my position, which was on a high overlook near the road to Vultee Arch. I could see for many miles. I estimated that there were at least twenty military jet aircraft of jet-fighter to commercial-airliner size, flying at altitudes of 7,000 to 20,000 feet. My campsite elevation was about 4,600 feet.

Then things really got interesting and I ended up staying up the entire night, as did the Loy Butte witnesses who were four miles to the west of me. At 8:35 p.m. two fighters flying in formation in the northeast at about 10,000 feet were fired at from the southeast. The "shot" came from below the jets and looked very much like a meteorite, but this went up, not down. Minutes later two other jet fighters were making a wide banking turn at about 8,000 feet near Secret Canyon. These two jets were fired at by something I could not see above and to the northwest. In both cases the jets did not change course or take any defensive or offensive action that I could see. The same applied to all the other jets. They all just seemed to be waiting and watching something. Those shots, or whatever they were, seemed to me to be warnings, like firing a shot over the bow of a ship. Keep in mind that the crews of these jet aircraft, which could have included as many as one hundred pilots and navigators or more, obviously knew in detail what was going on that night.

What I witnessed that night is of inestimable significance to us commoners, but we are being kept in the dark by our own country-men. Why? Is government fear of panic and retribution that great? I doubt it. I think there is more to it than that. And if these pilots and crews were briefed on what was going on, there are probably a thousand more who are in on this thing, including the entire subject of aliens and UFOs in general.

At 8:40 p.m., as I was intently watching jets, I was looking northeast. I turned to look to the west and there, at about 8,000 feet, was an object of tremendous size flying from west to east. It was moving at about 200 mph and made no sound at all. This object, or craft, had the general pattern of a round cluster of white lights and several red lights. All of these lights moved in perfect unison across the clear night sky. They seemed to be attached to a huge, dark craft the size and shape of which I could not determine even in bright moonlight. In a state of absolute awe, I watched the huge object fly to the north of Capitol Butte and then right over the center of Sedona. I asked numerous local residents if they had seen anything unusual in the sky that night and most replied that they had been watching television.

I turned to look to the far west from where the craft had come. There, brightly illuminated by moonlight on the north side of Secret Mountain, was a billowing, towering column of white smoke about 1,000 feet high and approximately 500 feet wide. Smoke at the base of this growing column was caught in a breeze and was drifting across the top of Secret Mountain to the south for over half a mile. I did not see a flash and did not hear an explosion, but the column of white smoke must have been connected with the strange craft with red and white lights that had just passed over Secret Mountain.

Several weeks prior to this August 23rd incident there had been a forest fire on Secret Mountain that had burned for ten days and had charred over 2,000 acres of Ponderosa pine and scrub oak forest. The fire is of extremely suspicious origin and circumstance. Jet fighters, helicopters and UFOs figure strongly in this event. It took about an hour for the smoke from the explosion (or implosion) to disperse.

I was so engrossed in and fascinated by what I was watching that I never even gave a thought to the camera and audio recording equipment I had sitting in a case several feet away, prepared for just such an event. The jets gradually thinned out and by 10:00 p.m. only an occasional airliner was flying overhead. Hours passed like minutes that night. And then suddenly, at 10:52 p.m., an incredible sphere of blazing chrome-white light descended out of the sky in the west, high over Secret Mountain. This sphere became brighter and brighter as it descended. It slowed, and as it did it became dimmer and dimmer and then blinked out entirely exactly in the center of where the towering pillar of white smoke had been over Secret Mountain. If this light had landed it would have come down on the exact center, the "ground zero," of the mysterious explosion of a few

Figure 1.   Photo of UFOs on the same night the smoke column was seen. See photo/drawing on opposite page.

hours earlier.

Then, at 11:15 p.m., through my binoculars I watched an air-craft with a red and a green light and a white strobe light fly at slow speed north to south over the same area of the earlier smoke pillar on Secret Mountain. At 11:25 p.m. a sphere of chrome-white light identical to the one I saw a half-hour earlier flew very slowly, south to north, on the same flight path the aircraft had taken.

I finally remembered the camera and thoroughly chastised my-self for being so stupid and negligent, but better late than never, I thought. So I put the camera, a Minolta X-370 SLR with 1600-speed film, in a spot where I could grab it in an instant. Feeling increasingly drowsy and thinking that the action was probably over, I lay down on the bed in my camper but kept my eyes on Secret Mountain through the back windows. I began dozing off and finally fell asleep.

Some minutes later my eyes snapped open almost automat-ically. I looked at Maroon Mountain, which is just to the north side of Secret Mountain. Two blazing spheres of chrome-white lights skimmed across the top of Maroon Mountain and flew in a graceful curving formation straight in my direction.

In one electrified instant I grabbed the camera and stumbled out of the van barefoot and dressed only in a pair of hiking shorts. I was overwhelmed with fear and fascination as the lights came rapidly closer. The beauty of those chrome-white lights is impossible to

Top of Secret Mt.
(about one mile)

There were no clouds in the sky
that night — there was a full moon

Pillar of explosion smoke
1000 feet high

Secret Canyon
(not visible)

Lighter/thinner smoke drifting across
the top of Secret Mountain

Maroon Mountain

Figure 2.   Drawing of area where smoke column was seen.

describe accurately. I have never seen anything like it. They came closer and closer and then stopped and hovered a short distance from where I stood. They began to dim rapidly and I snapped a photo. The camera jammed. A top-of-the-line Minolta that has never given me a bit of trouble jammed as two UFOs hovered right in front of me, as if giving me a perfect shot. My heart sank and I remember thinking that the whole thing was right out of a Steven Spielberg movie. A scriptwriter couldn't have done it better than this.

Then the lights blinked out. "They" were right there, sitting out there in the dark, but I could not see them. I looked all around, behind, above, both sides. I could not see them but I knew they were there. And what were they going to do? I thought, "This is it — and no witnesses." I took up my note pad and quickly scribbled in large letters this message: "12:10 a.m. two brilliant balls of light coming straight in my direction — flew over Maroon Mountain." If I disappeared for a while or for good, at least there would be a note. The Travis Walton experience was heavy on my mind in those moments.

The next day, while fiddling with the camera, I discovered that a thin plastic ring liner just behind the lens opening had come loose and had gotten stuck in the mirror of the camera, jamming the mirror in the open position, blocking the viewfinder and locking the shutter. As it turns out, the photo I took came out anyway, although it was taken at a time when the lights were a tiny fraction of their flying brightness. But at least it was something.

At that point, I got fully dressed and prepared to stay up the rest of the night. There was no way I was going to try to sleep. Then things took a different, even stranger turn. At 12:30 a.m. a carload of drunken Mexicans pulled off the road several hundred yards away and opened the car doors so that everything within two miles could hear trumpets and accordion music blasting from their car stereo. They must have had speakers three feet high in that car. This sort of thing normally infuriates me, but that night I welcomed the company and noise. They were drinking and shouting until 4:00 a.m. Maybe the UFO will get them instead, I thought. The loud music woke a man sleeping in a late-model white Jeep Cherokee between me and the Mexicans. He started the motor, turned on the headlights and then drove around the desert erratically for ten minutes. He seemed to find a better spot four or five times before he finally just drove away in the direction of Sedona. Extremely odd behavior, it seemed.

At almost the same time the UFOs had blinked out and the Mexicans had arrived, I had heard a tremendous crashing in the brush to my left about 150 feet away. The crashing continued steadily but the music was so loud it almost drowned out the crashing and snapping sounds in the dry piñon pine and manzanita. Those of us who spend a lot of time in the high desert know how tough manzanita bushes are. The one- to two-inch trunks and limbs are like iron and when the limbs break they leave jagged edges.

Three things had begun happening almost simultaneously: the Mexicans, the white Jeep and the crashing in the brush. At about 12:45 a.m. I realized that whatever was in the brushy forest was of extreme weight. It sounded like three or four thousand-pound steers, all plowing through heavy brush. That's what cattle do. If they are going somewhere, they go through things, not around them. But then I remembered that there hadn't been any cattle in that particular area for a long time. As I listened to the crashing slowly moving away from me I realized that something was highly out of the ordinary. There was too much crashing too continuously. A cow would stop and graze or moo or something, but there was just this steady, linear, heavy crashing of brush, with the sounds receding from where I was.

I stood there wondering why in the hell it's always me who sees this stuff and has these kinds of experiences. I have four, soon to be five, widely distributed books full of these types of occurrences. Many of these unusual incidents and experiences were witnessed by at least one other adult individual.

I became so engrossed by whatever was making the crashing sounds that for a while I completely forgot about the UFOs. With my big six-volt flashlight I walked across a wide, sandy clearing to the area where I had first heard the crashing sounds. I cautiously made my way a short distance into the pines and manzanitas. Although the moon was directly overhead and bright, I unavoidably stepped on some twigs I did not see. The crashing sounds, about 100 yards away at that point, stopped. Whatever it was, it was now watching me. I was on a higher ridge and the tallest pines below were up to ten feet high but sparse enough so that I should have been able to see what it was that was doing the crashing. I turned on the powerful flashlight and shone the beam all around down below in the area where I had last heard brush snapping. I couldn't see anything out of the ordinary.

In the unlikely event it was deer, the only nondomestic animal heavy enough to perhaps make such sounds, they would get curious and look at the light and I would see their shining eyes reflected. But I saw no eyes and no cow or deer silhouette and I heard no sound. I switched the light off and reasoned that it just had to be cattle. As I walked away the heavy crashing of brush slowly and cautiously resumed and then slowly faded away to the southwest.

I went back to the van and waited up the rest of the night. Nothing else of an unusual nature happened that night.

At first light I searched the area of the crashing brush sounds. In the dry dusty soil there were no fresh tracks of any kind except for those of one medium-sized deer, which would have weighed no more than 100 pounds. During the night the deer had passed through the gully nonstop on its way somewhere. It was not the maker of the sounds. What made the crashing noises? I have not the slightest idea what it was. The next day I learned that a local rancher has had this same experience several times near his ranch.

As a result of what I (and two others) saw that Tuesday night, August 23, 1994, my life has not been and never again will be the same. We all might take a more serious view of UFO activities, particularly as they now concern and involve all of us. I think too many people still put UFOs into the entertainment category.

Just after completing the above, I learned that on Tuesday, August 16, 1994, at 8:40 p.m., two prominent Sedona business owners had watched the same huge white-and-red-lit object I had seen on Tuesday, August 23. In this sighting the craft flew north to south over Sedona at a very high speed and was being chased, unsuccessfully, by two jet fighters.

At 10:00 p.m., Thursday, August 25, 1994, I was visiting at a friend's house in the Quail Hollow subdivision. Suddenly the house, brand new and large, began to vibrate violently. It took us a few seconds to realize that there were helicopters over the roof of the house. The helicopters were moving fast. We grabbed a pair of binoculars and ran out onto the back deck. The moon was just rising in the northeast and it silhouetted the helicopters perfectly. With the binoculars, we got a good look at them. They were flying at roof-top height. The lead helicopter had one red light underneath, but the two following helicopters were completely dark — no lights on at all. FAA-approved?

We later discussed the fact that it seemed as though they were chasing something, but we didn't see what it might have been. As it turns out, a group of local witnesses saw what the military helicopters were indeed chasing. These people were at Posse Grounds Park. This is high ground that overlooks most of Sedona. They heard the helicopters coming from the south and turned to look in that direction. Two spheres of blue light flew past them at high speed about 100 feet above the ground. The lights were about a foot in diameter and might have been attached to a larger, darker object. The lights were about a quarter of a mile ahead of the helicopters.

The balls of blue light went across the city of Sedona and up Schnebly Hill. Schnebly Hill is actually a wide, steep canyon. The lights made a U-turn halfway up Schnebly Hill and then disappeared to the east. The helicopters (it's not known what model they were) continued straight up Oak Creek Canyon and then over the 6,000-foot Mogollon Rim above Sedona. This whole incident lasted for no more than 60 to 90 seconds.

Battle in the Sky — What Really Happened

Zoosh through Robert Shapiro
August 24, 1994

*T*om came in all excited. He had actually seen — not heard about from someone, but seen — a humongous UFO! There were jets in groups. There were what looked something like tracer bullets going across to the jet planes like warning shots. Something was dropped on top of Secret Mountain and it created a column of smoke but no sound. There were UFOs everywhere. He said it was just awesome! I'd like to know who the participants were and what they were doing. Then broaden it a little bit.

Well now, you know that the base in Secret Mountain has had multiple uses. Not only is it the clandestine secret government base, but also you must remember that the shadow government has strange bedfellows as partners, as they say in politics. Not to be too alarmist, but known political, physical beings, Earth beings, terrorists, have occasionally frequented that base — not on the secure levels of the base but on the upper levels. So sometimes the mischief they are involved in creates a little annoyance.

Sometimes there are training exercises. What was seen in the sky was *not* a training exercise. This is the time now of all-out war between these extraterrestrials who would attempt to liberate your planet from the — how can we say — more structured elements that would control you, all right?

So he was seeing something that was a battle. But he was also seeing something that was somewhat layered. After all, the powers that be would be quite clear that there would be many eyewitnesses to this event. It wasn't exactly something that was clandestine in its appearance.

So the event — one moment, you have to excuse me, there is a radiation being beamed from that particular area and that radiation is designed to create an envelope of security around that base. It is not really intended to cause interference with spiritual activities, but it does have that effect and that effect is known. This particular signal that is being broadcast is intended to interfere with the way ships from other planets operate. Those who broadcast that beacon know that the energy that ships use, advanced ships as well as the ones that are more conventional, is the same energy that people use for spiritual atonement. So when people who are in and around Sedona have some difficulty with their spiritual activities, they might be using a similar frequency for their spiritual activities.

Tom felt that what he saw last night was a war, a battle. Who were the participants and what was happening? What can you tell us about all this?

This was thinly disguised. Some people hope that from a distance, people might assume this was a war game. Of course, if you were sufficiently close up, you would be able to make out some details. As you know, the ETs that we have been calling the pirates do not have a big ship. There is a big ship involved, as you have indicated, so it can only be either an ally of the pirates or, what I believe is more likely, someone who is attempting to combat the secret government directly. Remember I said a while back there was a discussion to . . .

To rescind the prime directive, and they have done that, right?

Yes. Although, this rescinding of the noninterference policy has allowed wider parameters of action, it does not mean that ETs are going to come in and take over. It does mean that they might come in, as in this last case, and act on overt acts toward them. This means that if they are interfered with in the pursuit of peaceful activities, they can retaliate. This is not an unknown factor in military factions, even in this world, where the more significant powers feel that it is their right to overfly any country they wish, as long as they are not doing anything destructive. So it is a similar attitude with the ETs, who will overfly very closely and even scan the bases and . . .

Are they positive ETs, though?

Yes, positive. But in some cases, there are those who have the capacity to be warlike also. You must remember that positive ETs who are totally positive and spiritual beings cannot make war as you know it. So they have to recruit people who can, but who will work toward the best end and are in their own right incorruptible. As you know, many warriors, especially from some ancient cultures, are incorruptible. Where do you find warriors like this, you might ask.

In ancient Orion?

You might think that they would exist in ancient Orion, yes; however, in this case they did not. They needed to have people who were absolutely aware that they would evolve into very benevolent beings. They also needed to have people who, if one of the ETs were captured, could not be manipulated in any way against anyone else. An ancient Orion warrior might possibly be manipulated against his own people, but I won't say how. So they had to go to another source.

They traveled back in time, asked for volunteers and came up with ancient warriors from the Pleiades. It might interest you to know that these people wore breastplates very similar to the one Joan of Arc is pictured wearing. I might add that this is where the idea came from.

Now, these breastplates are largely for decoration, but they do have a protective element and that element is to protect the emotional center from the harm that would be caused by other people's violent thoughts. So, their warlike response is in equal opposition to that which is directed toward them. That's different from the Orion warriors who can generate their own warlike response. The ancient Pleiadian warriors always and only would equally reflect that which is sent to them. It is very safe, you see, to use this type of person as a warrior, because if they are confronted with someone trying to kill them, they can defend themselves.

But they won't initiate it?

That's correct. So that is what we are dealing with here, a Pleiadian warship. A few of the pirate vessels were there because the Pleiadians brought back these warriors from the ancient Pleiades. They have the ability to talk to the pirates. They haven't achieved it yet, but they are working toward achieving a peaceful agreement and an interim allied status between themselves and the pirates. When they do that, the pirates will no longer need to mine these premises, including the Moon.

They will give the pirates some other place to mine?

They will give them someplace else that is far away from here, and in this way, the Pleiadian warriors can deal directly with the shadow government without having too many other parties to negotiate with.

Who fights along with the shadow government? The Orions?

Only.

You said the Orions were miners and engineers?

That's right. But the shadow government has successfully alienated everybody, so they don't have many allies. They might have individuals, you understand, whom they have gotten entangled in the Earth system, but they don't have too many direct allies of a specific group. So you might get some corrupting beings. Right now, you have the advantage here. You have the advantage, Earth people, and that is that, as so often happens amongst groups of people who are greedy for something or other, there is a falling out. Contracts among the pirate element do not often hold because there is no cause other than greed or lust for power. There is no higher purpose as a result; the element of self-sacrifice to protect one's friends and fellow warriors is not present. That is the real reason these negative beings cannot win. That is why people such as Hitler attempted to create a cause through which he could create loyalty amongst the troops, but in the final analysis, it did not work. They still turned on each other.

Okay, so specifically last night, who owned the large ship? Was that the Pleiadians?

Yes.

What were the jet planes doing there? These were United States military. They did not seem to be doing anything except observing, but they were in groups of one, two, three and five.

They were as you say, observing. They knew enough not to get too involved, but there is also a certain amount of shadow government manipulation of the military. You know they can run kind of like a sequence of events in which the military will respond and not realize right off the bat that it is not their own bidding. So the jets were there because they felt that they were supposed to be there. They had been ordered to come, and yet when they arrived and saw what there was to see, they radioed back to their home base.

Which is?

I'm sorry, it's too close to reveal and they could suffer from the revelation. They were instructed to hold their position, observe and fire only if fired upon. So that is what they did. They were U.S. military jets.

What was the soundless bomb that hit on top of Secret Mountain and went up in a column of smoke?

This is an ultrasonic weapon. These weapons are actually in the experimental stage now on this planet. This weapon does not create an explosion as you know it, but when it is dropped, it expands using high-frequency sound waves. It goes into the target zone where it successfully disrupts and causes every machine there to simply go crazy and self-destruct. It is destructive also to all life forms there, and anything that could blow up or burn will do so. But the weapon itself does not create an explosion.

Who did it? Whose weapon was it?

This was a weapon designed and built in the ancient Pleiadian empires for use against predatory races. Even in those days they didn't use it on each other, but they would use it on predators. The way that ET cultures have been able to justify their actions now is by viewing various terrorist activities, either by the shadow government or by others, as predatory action.

What were they aiming at? What was the target? The base itself?

An opening into the base.

What was the result? What was the damage?

The damage, at least on the upper levels, was very serious and probably cannot be repaired. Now let me tell you another factor: As you know, the shadow government is abandoning that base and has largely moved out. But, depending upon your point of view, you might say they were very irresponsible, because they were willing to let various terrorists and pirate organizations just take over what was left. The Pleiadians were not willing to allow this to happen, so they destroyed most of the leftover equipment, especially the exotic equipment.

The shadow government was given certain ET technology that was designed to be a prototype from which they would build their own. But they kept the prototypes. They have built their own to the extent that they are able, and they have abandoned many of the prototypes. So these prototypes of very serious equipment were going to fall into the hands of people who were considerably less responsible. (This is a strange word to use in the case of the shadow government.) The shadow government is ultimately responsible; they do not wish to destroy the planet, for that is the culture that feeds them. Whereas certain terrorist groups or pirate groups, both ET and Earth-oriented, might be willing to see everything destroyed, because they feel that they have nothing to lose.

Specifically, what terrorist groups? Are they Earth-based?

They are Middle Eastern groups, but not the PLO or anything like that. The PLO is coming into its own.

Yes. It's becoming respectable.

They have always been a legitimate government. They were there first and they are now going to become established, so they ought to be recognized. But these are more fringe groups, what I would describe as groups that operate almost as a criminal element. Meaning that their initial motivations were political, but they have moved from the political into something similar to a criminal basis. You must remember that when people feel they have nothing to lose, they will be cavalier with the entire planet. So these terrorist groups, these terrorists, need to be nurtured back into the system.

Many Earth terrorists now are going to be taken up in UFOs. They are not going to have their political motivations taken away, but they will have their violent attitudes changed or transformed. As a gift, they will be given the means by which they also can transform their political situation for themselves, for their families and for their tribes in a way that is constructive. This means, for instance, that they might have their mental capacity greatly raised. Or they might have their inspirational level raised to the extent that they are given the opportunity to invent things that will help people, that will bring a great deal of money and recognition to their part of the world.

What is needed in that part of the world is not the development of natural resources, but the development of the people themselves to a point where they themselves are the resource. The U.S. has been doing this for a long time, what they call think tanks. The new think tanks will all be in the Middle East. This will be on a more benevolent basis, not only scientifically, but also philosophically and religiously. I bring this up because a lot of what is going on, even now as we speak, are lift-offs.

As a result of that weapon, some people, I am sorry to say, were killed. There was death there. Last night there was a loss of life of about thirteen individuals; about forty-three others were severely injured. Most of these were taken up to the ships to be taken care of.

To whose ship?

The Pleiadians' battleship. The Pleiadian warship.

It's humongous. How big is it?

Well, it is significant; it could be about ten miles across.

Is there only one of these or are there several?

There is just one. With your technology now, it is basically indestructible. It is also incorruptible because of where it is from and, more importantly, *when* it's from. It has one other ship within itself that is about three miles across. In any event, lots of other little ships can be discharged, too. There are many little ships because, of course, the main ship is not going to be involved directly unless it is absolutely necessary.

In any event, this main battle is over. I do not know if there will be any others. Your military knows what is going on, but they are powerless to interfere. This is part of the reason that there is such a blackout and secrecy. Can you imagine your military saying, "Well, fellow Americans, there is a war going on on our soil and we are powerless to prevent it"? It is not the sort of thing they would feel comfortable saying, but they really are powerless to prevent it.

Is this why they are publicizing this health plan and the Simpson trial all over the news — just to cover up?

No, that is another story.

Are you saying that the actual shadow government and the ETs have left the base outside of Sedona?

Yes.

They moved out when? We haven't seen any black helicopters for a couple of weeks.

They have been out for about a week and a half. Now, you might still see vestiges of what you identify their people to have, the black helicopters and so on. But there are some genuine black helicopters involved in your own military service used for so-called night activities. I would say that your base with the shadow government is not there anymore.

And the negative ETs are all gone?

Yes.

But you can't tell me where they went?

They went to the place that is hidden in plain sight.

With all their flying craft?

Yes. It is masked in plain sight. It is probably the best way to do it.

Let's back up a little bit. Who specifically went to get the Pleiadians? Who went back in time to get them?

The Pleiadian representative on the galactic council was the one. I don't like using those terms because they have been so overused in recent years, but this is a galactic council that oversees the development of cultures and civilizations in this part of the universe.

Where are they headquartered?

They are located beyond the range of any weapons. They are located right around the point of unfoldment of your galaxy, in roughly what would appear to you to be the center of your galaxy. It is a fairly safe place because the center of any galaxy is a place where life is being formed. With the slightest motion, they can move beyond the veil into another dimension.

Is this at the edge of what we call the black hole, which you say to call the white hole?

Yes.

Are they in charge of all of the beneficial ET ships that are around the planet right now? Who is doing the green fire balls and all of that?

I don't want to say that they are in charge, but they gave permission for a coordinated effort to take place.

Well, who then around the planet is basically in charge?

Your future selves are in charge. You see, it has to be someone with a stake in this matter. It has to be someone who loves the people here on Earth. It has to be someone who has a soul connection to your culture. It has to be someone who will not become involved in the squabbles and political infighting that are present in every person, whether spiritual, rational or irrational, in your now time. Who else could qualify?

How can we describe them so that they fit into literature that we have read or that we know? What are they called?

They would appear to be humans. You can call them humans.

So you are saying that there is a soul aspect of most of the people on the planet up there in those ships? Or a connection to the monad? You say future self but . . .

The next level of your spiritual evolution is these people.

Is that why Arthur [Fanning] kept seeing pictures of all those people in councils running around and talking? Was it some part of him that is there he was tuning in to?

He has the ability to view things at a distance. Yes, there is one of his reincarnational selves there in a position from which he can watch.

So there was a lot of activity, a lot of rushing around?

He is experiencing second sight.

There is a disturbance there. Let me talk about that a minute. As a result of this activity, there is a disturbance in the fabric of time in that part of your land now, where that base was. This disturbance will create a ripple effect there that will last, in your time sequence and the time sequence you are traveling through, for about three and one-half months of your experiential time. I cannot underline this enough. *Going into that area on foot, in a vehicle, even flying low through that area in a helicopter or in a small plane, is extremely dangerous.* It has created an effect similar to that of the Bermuda Triangle. At times it might be possible to walk right through and feel no particular thing; at other times, you walk through, come out, go back to your car and it's not there! And you wonder, where is my car? Then you think, boy, it is a long walk back to town! You start walking back to town and you'll say, where are the houses, the land looks different. You will come to where the town is, and you might see a dinosaur!

It is possible to walk right through a hole in time there and not even have the slightest hint, not even be dizzy. Normally, in a time window that is naturally created, there is a physical effect so you will know something happened, and you can find your way back. But this is an artificial situation, so I must say, please be careful.

There is also a time portal set there that is essentially a vacuum. It functions like a vacuum you use on your carpets; it is designed to pick up warriors, both ET and otherwise, transport them immediately to a ship for processing, and then send them to their proper places. Many of them will have all memory of this event and events of the past three years erased not only from their minds, but also from the cellular memory of their bodies so they would have no way (short of spiritual, which would include dreams) of recalling the event.

So I would say don't go there. I know people are going to want to. You can get close, but it is really, really unsafe to go into the immediate area. If you have to get close, bring telescopes; that's safe. You can bring cameras with long-range lenses; that is also safe. But don't go in there if you can possibly help it. Now, a few people who don't know will just wander in there. There may be means to protect them, but maybe not. I can just say that I hope that everyone will be safe.

Then after three and one-half months that will be dissipated?

It will gradually dissipate over three and one-half months. Right now it is a big hole. Very unsafe. Extremely unstable.

Right now the date is 24 August 1994. So what is the future of that base? The damage was such that you can't get into the lower levels now?

It is not likely that you can access the lower levels, but if anybody was in the lower levels, they are probably all right. I am not saying that there is anybody there, but if anybody could get in, it would be fine. But you couldn't get out the old way. You would have to go someplace else. And after you went someplace else, you might then be able to get out, but it is highly questionable. As far as ETs go, they are allowed. The only people who might be down there might be some people who chose to stay. Let me look at the lower levels. No, I see no sign of life as you know it. All corridors are sealed externally. There is a means of access, but that access cannot be attained from the surface.

All right, so that is this base?

Yes.

That is one of, I think we had said five plus three inactive; Dulce is inactive, Denver is inactive and Iceland is inactive at the moment.

Yes, I am not counting that.

Okay, so what is this Pleiadian ship going to do to the bases at the North and South Poles, and to the one at the Cape of Good Hope?

Now that they've essentially made an example of this base, they might be able to start negotiating. The shadow government feels it is relatively impervious. They were able to get out of this base, but they will not miss the point, which is to say that all defensive systems to the contrary, this ET ship was able to penetrate it just like a hot knife through butter. Very easy. That point will not be lost on them.

So the misfire that started the fire in Sedona a couple of weeks ago, was that the same Pleiadian ship? Was that what caused the shadow government to get out? Was that an attack?

I don't think that was the Pleiadian ship. For one thing, it would have been too irresponsible for them. When they use their weapons, they generally hit what they are aiming at.

Okay, evidently there was some damage and then there was a misfire. Can you look into that for us?

I believe that might have been a pirate ship. And it wasn't a misfire. We are talking essentially about the ship itself being damaged while it was in the act of firing. That is what created the misfire. It wasn't just a dumb mistake.

There were no beneficial ships around at that time, then?

Yes, there were, but . . .

They were not involved?

That's right. You can't always prevent everything.

Is the event that started the fire, what led to the decision to abandon the base?

No, the decision to do that had already been made.

Is there anything else we need to know about this war and what is going on in other parts of the world?

No, this is not likely to affect too many Earth people because the weapons that are being used on both sides are not the same kinds of weapons that are used in conventional warfare. Casualties that happen as a result of conventional warfare are not going to be much of a factor. In any war such as in the so-called Desert Storm, a minimum of 80% of the casualties are innocent people who just happen to be there. This is not going to be the case.

So this might accelerate the whole process, then, and we might not have to wait until year 2002. Will this accelerate it?

It cannot do that, you see, because you need time. It is like when you fry an egg; even if everybody is ready to eat, the egg still has to be cooked. So you might not be ready as individuals. You are probably going to be waiting until that time, although you may see some effects. Hopefully, you will see some beneficial effects, but regardless, your souls, your bodies must be able to go through what they need to go through to get to that stage. Also, there are other potentials happening on the spirit level. I can't talk about it too much because if I do, it will disrupt it. But I will say that there is help, there is hope.

So we might not have to go as deep into the control and the manipulation by the shadow government as was earlier predicted?

Let's hope not.

Another Sedona Sighting

Anonymous

Excerpted from a transcription of a June
phone call to Tom Dongo

It was early March. I know this for a fact because a friend of mine
went to Phoenix to see the the Grateful Dead. He was returning to
Sedona with some friends and we were all going to camp out. I was
already at the campground, in the main pool with five or six people,
and more people were camped down the hill. All of us witnessed this
event! We were sitting around the fire playing guitar. There were no
drugs around us, so this was not a hallucination.

We looked up at the sky, and right above us, taking up the
whole area high in the sky was a huge ship! I am estimating that it
was about twice the size of an aircraft carrier. I am an artist, so I have
a good sense of relative size. It was triangular in shape, like the letter
L flying. One side of it was long and the other side was short. From
the tops of the long line and the short line, you could draw a line
down joining the two points. I have done some technical illustrating
so I know that that is not proper aerodynamics. This object made
absolutely no noise. We couldn't make out details except that it was
gray and stood out from the dark sky at each point. There were three
red globe-like lights.

It was a very clear night and we watched this object fly all the
way into the wilderness area above Schnebly Hill. It was going to the

right and it was moving fast. It was huge. It blotted out star patterns. Blotted them out. Unbelievable!

Would you estimate the length to be three to four hundred yards?

I couldn't estimate because the object was so high up, but I would say that it was definitely larger than two aircraft carriers. We walked back to the campfire and saw another one! We watched that one fly off. Then we turned back and saw another one! Three of them, all together. After that, there were two aircraft that made noise. These objects had made no noise. Two aircraft were very high, but we could hear the the aircraft wailing, trying to keep up. Then we realized that those little specks of planes could have landed on them, taken off, landed on them and taken off again. That is how huge it was. And they could probably have parked and gotten lost in the thing.

Did they sound like jet fighters?

No, there was no sound when those ships were overhead. It was during a span of ten minutes that we saw the first ship, the second ship, the third ship. Then the jets trailed them by quite some time.

Since the '60s there has been a lot they aren't telling us. I know that for a fact. There is more to the Russian wall falling down and everything else than meets the eye. I think it's a technological coup d'état. This is just my own opinion.

The next morning three people camped on a ridge came down to where we were and said, "Did you see that?" We all confirmed it. Two businessmen from Atlanta had been with us all along. Before they left, I drew the ship and I said, "Did it look like this? Did it blot out stars? Was it solid or were there just lights in that pattern?"

"No, it was solid." We cleared this up.

There was talk in town. A bunch of people were up there the next night, UFO-watching. After that, guess what? There were maneuvers, jet maneuvers with their high beams and their lights. They were pulling out, doing wild stuff, and then trying to line up in the L-shaped pattern, but you could see the stars. I kept trying to tell the people, "No, this isn't it."

I took two days off from work after this because I could not comprehend it or deal with it. And of course, I don't know what it means. A mothership. Does that mean they are going to beam everyone up and leave us behind if some catastrophe comes? What's going on? Do the rumors about the Hopi and the Mayan prophecies include being beamed up? I don't know.

I did not tell this to a whole lot of people. There are only about three people I could discuss this with, other than the people who witnessed it, who would understand. I didn't tell anybody at work, but a friend of mine had told me once about an experience. At the time I listened to him with an open mind, but I kind of disbelieved his experience. I ran into him and told him about this event. He asked what night it had occurred, and we pinpointed it.

He said he'd been camped out near a road that goes from Boynton Canyon to Red Canyon. Out that way, there is a little gully with some trees where he parks. He was awakened at about two-thirty in the morning — he looked at his clock — and there were a bunch of white trucks, all-white tractor-trailers with no markings. They were not cattle trucks. He didn't follow them. He was spooked. He woke up and had to hike down the road about a quarter of a mile before he could see them. He just kept hearing them rolling. Finally, he counted twelve trucks. It kind of made me think about this event and wonder if they were related. And then the crash here happened a little after that.

Were the tractor-trailers the box type?

They were white tractor trailers. They had black numbers and coded letters or whatever on the back and that was it. Nothing else.

9

UFOs, ETs and More

by Tom Dongo
September 20, 1994

I want to thank the many readers who have written and expressed great interest and support in my writing about UFOs, aliens and the paranormal. It can be, and often is, an infernally frustrating business in many ways. And thank you too, for all the interesting personal experiences you have sent to me.

Sedona really is, in a paranormal sense, an extraordinary and unusual place. Sedona is likely a neutral zone between time and dimensions, a portal area that allows all sorts of things to enter — or to go back and forth. This includes numerous varieties of flying crafts and their crews. I think it also includes a few lower, questionably intelligent creatures that have an ability to materialize and dematerialize in the general Sedona area. In the last four months there has been almost continuous supernormal activity, some of which is difficult to rationalize with conventional terminology. I am presently involved in an investigation, very tangible, that is in the purest sense supernormal or supernatural. It is in no way negative. It probably has little to do with UFOs or UFO aliens. To protect identities and locations I am not going to be more specific. This activity, from what I've seen, falls, directly into the realms of the extreme paranormal. I hope to get four or five or more good photographs for my research.

On September 12 about 8:30 p.m. I witnessed something quite unusual, and I wasn't the only one. A Sedona woman saw the same objects that I did, but from a different, and apparently better, vantage point. She was a mile or so east of me, which gave her a clearer view than I had. As astonishing as this sighting was, no one else seems to have observed it.

As I was gazing toward the north at the night sky, I caught a glimpse of odd lights heading in my direction. I lost sight of them, but I mentally plotted their trajectory and watched where they should appear. To my amazement, a cluster of red-and-white lights appeared, and seconds later a second cluster appeared several hundred yards behind the first. These two clusters had the general shape of a triangle and silently circled the city of Sedona three times at an altitude of about 3000 feet. On the second and third passes I snapped a half-dozen photos, one of which is printed below.

Two Xpotaz UFOs

There has been enough UFO and other unusual activity in the Sedona area in the past four months to give me fuel for a long-term investigation. I received the following letter in the mail the other day, which typifies what has been transpiring here lately. Without a doubt Sedona is again the world's hot spot for UFO activity. The letter follows, and I thank Dana for sending it.

Dear Tom,

Greetings! Let me first express my appreciation for the thorough and informative research you have done, as evidenced by your books, which I have found to be very compelling, exciting and thought-provoking.

I wanted to share a mysterious experience/sighting I had on the night of Wednesday, August 31st. I figure you must have had other reports regarding the same occurrence and probably have an idea of what actually took place. I for one am baffled, and if my report can simply serve to reinforce or duplicate someone else's report, then my mission is accomplished.

Between 7:45 pm and 8:00 p.m., on the night of August 31st, I was driving east out Jacks Canyon Road from the Village of Oak Creek. The sun had already disappeared behind the horizon to the west, and the sky was getting dark. As I looked out my front car window in a northeastern direction, I noticed a strange pinkish cloud above and beyond Lee Mountain. I could not figure out how this cloud was illuminated, as the sky was getting too dark and the other clouds over the western horizon weren't getting any light from the setting sun. Suddenly I saw this pink cloud light up (from within or below) in a bright yellow flash that lasted perhaps a full second or two, then faded. There was no lightning activity in the night sky at all. I pulled over and continued my observation out of the car.

My first thought was that something had exploded or crashed on the ground. However, approximately 30 seconds later, this flash of light occurred again and again and again in about 30-second intervals for about 30 minutes! Within 15 minutes of my first sighting of this event, in the sky over this area (approximately 10 miles from my position) I counted eight flying craft, which I suspected were helicopters because of the stationary positions the red and white lights were assuming in the night sky. I then noticed two pairs of red and white lights in formation flying from the area in my direction, banking to circle and return to the area of activity. These lights looked like wing-tip lights on two jet aircraft surveying the scene.

I thought that I might get to a closer vantage point if I drove out to Interstate 17 and headed north toward Flagstaff to the overlook area. This I proceeded to do, and approximately 25 minutes later I was there, only to discover no more aircraft in the sky. The flashing light had apparently moved to a position farther northeast of my position, northeast of Stoneman Lake. I returned home not knowing any more about this event.

What Dana probably should have done, if possible, was pull off the road and from there watch the activity over Lee Mountain. I don't know how many times I have driven farther in an effort to find a better vantage point only to find the object, or objects, gone when I got closer. Sometimes you have to grab the opportunity as it is — because often it may only last seconds, or minutes at best. A pair of binoculars and even an inexpensive point-and-shoot camera carried in the car is a great asset in an active UFO area. Often a distant object on a three-by-five 200 or 400 ASA supermarket photo print can be enlarged with stunning results. High-speed film does not usually work well because high-speed (1000 ASA or above) is just too grainy for good enlargements.

I have recently watched large and small aircraft change running lights into different patterns in a seeming effort to look like a UFO or something else. Why? I have also seen what I think was a huge UFO trying to look like a very large jet aircraft. The craft, however, made no sound whatsoever. A number of people have seen that around here. I have also seen jet fighters flying in a manner that to me strongly suggested they were expecting or were ready for an attack. An attack by whom or what in U.S. airspace?

A week ago, on the night of September 13, during a wild series of UFO sightings, I saw what looked to be a small, probably twin-engine plane coming toward me at a low altitude. With only the naked eye it simply looked like a small plane making an approach to the Sedona airport with its landing lights on. But when I picked up my binoculars and looked at it, it was a different sight altogether. In the middle, on the underside of the plane, was a red, flashing strobe light. To the right and left of the strobe and what would be the middle of a light plane's wings, were two bright landing lights. But on the outer edge of each wing was a light that slowly pulsed with such a blazing brightness that at the peak of each pulse all you could see was the red strobe and a small inner portion of the "landing lights." It then turned east and flew right over Sedona. A UFO trying to look like a plane or a plane trying to look like a UFO? Whatever it was, it wasn't normal.

To make matters even more interesting, from the same general direction that the "twin-engine plane" approached, appeared two moving red lights in the distance. These lights were at first a pinpoint, but as they moved closer I got a clear look at them through my binoculars. These two lights, or spheres, were a deep crimson red and pulsed at intervals of about three seconds. They would each pulse separately: a long bright pulse, a diminishing brightness, a three-second or so pause and then the same long bright pulse lasting about five seconds.

I would estimate the diameter of each sphere at approximately two feet. They may have been much smaller or much larger, because I had no frame of reference such as trees or a mountaintop. These two lights flew in tandem and pulsed at exactly the same rate, although separately, and were moving at a speed of what I would judge to be between 80–100 mph. The two objects stayed close to each other, but slightly altered their relative position to one another as they flew, and disappeared behind a low mountain to the east.

At about that same time, west of Sedona a number of witnesses saw two white glowing UFOs followed at a distance by a jet fighter. One of the UFOs made a sharp reverse turn and headed straight for the fighter as if it were playing chicken with the fighter. Just before it would have hit the fighter the UFO made an abrupt 90-degree turn to the east and disappeared. This sort of thing, or something similar, has been seen a number of times around here. It almost seems like tempers are getting a bit short.

10

The Last Chance for Redemption

Zoosh through Robert Shapiro
September 13, 1994

*G*ood morning. *We've got a couple of little mysteries for you. The first one: Tom Brokaw, on NBC evening news September 8, 1994, reported a shaft of light traveling along the West Coast followed by a sonic boom. He commented that maybe the government would tell us about it in forty-seven years. What was it?*

The Government's New Light Ship

You understand the significance of the "forty-seven years" joke. It is definitely an insider's joke, and this man is witty. Remember that lesser lights, as well as those that are not seen, represent the testing of a new secret government vehicle. It is an interesting vehicle because they are now getting into the technology that takes them past simple flights to the Moon and so on. They're getting into technology that requires organic Light metamorphosis so that the vehicle can travel not only in Light – light speed and so on – but there must be a certain spiritual resonance with all that is around it at any moment, whether it is a fly or a mosquito or a bird or a planet. It must be in resonance spiritually.

That's how that's done, by the way, because when you are flying that fast, you can't get out of the way. It's like noticing a bird up ahead, and you're going to fly through it. You have to be able to fly through the bird in a way that does not harm it. True light speed is not the miles per second but when the vehicle itself becomes Light.

When this happens, it can travel through anything without harming it. Right now, as we speak, there are light speeds beyond light speed moving as Light, vehicles all around us that can travel through you, right through your body and do you no harm whatsoever, perhaps making you feel better when they have passed through.

They have begun testing this technology. Now, it's not as if someone in their branch does not read this material, but I'm going to tell you anyway. They think that they can test and utilize this material and be untouched by it. But as they will discover with every one of their test pilots, they will all have to maintain at least a certain level of calmness. I'll tell you how they're going to do this: Their test pilots will be trained in meditation so that they can maintain the perfect alpha wave while they are in flight. Because they must be perfectly calm, they must be segregated from the stresses of normal life every pilot faces, especially one who works for the shadow government. They are not fools; they realize that to operate such a craft, pilots will have to transform themselves spiritually. They know they cannot operate vehicles like this, Light vehicles, and do any intentional act of violence. They hope that by creating a brigade of pilots like this, they will perform tests for them that are not violent, but supportive.

Supportive of their purpose.

Yes. They hope to deceive the pilots of their true purpose. They are still naive. It is hard to imagine someone as crafty as this being naive, and yet they are, because they do not understand that once a person and the vehicle merge — because they must merge to travel in Light — it is not possible for this pilot or the ship to be deceived. Let us never forget that.

Let us simply say, without revealing too much, that this gift of this vehicle was given by individuals who knew the shadow government needed to make a step. And they didn't want to force the shadow government into making a sudden step into the Light because it would destroy them. It is, isn't it, reassuring to know that the ultimate upliftment of the shadow government itself will not be done through destructive means? When you think about it, it can't be. It has to be done through love, through ordination, through initiation, through all of the processes everyone goes through as they achieve their highest spiritual self integrated into their daily self. This is how it must happen.

This tells you somewhat how they receive this vehicle, does it not, from representatives of the angelic kingdom?

Specifically, who?

I am constrained. I will only say, specifically, the angelic individuals that have to do with travel and communication.

All right. Where do they build the ship, at one of the underground bases?

No. They don't have the capacity to build that ship. The ship was brought . . .

Oh, it was given to them.

Intact, yes. It was given to them. You know, when it solidifies, other than looking very streamlined and exotic, it does not look that much different on the inside than any other airworthy vehicle, though it doesn't have gauges and dials as one might expect in an airplane. It looks basically like any other flying ship, although it's more — well, how can we say it? — it's something that if you looked at it, you'd say it was the new model and you couldn't wait to have it.

What shape is it? I mean, does it look like a jet plane or like a triangular UFO?

It's an ellipse. That's why I say it's streamlined. It's basically rounded and thin.

The sonic boom. I thought these craft usually didn't make noise.

It was a low-speed test.

So how does the shadow government see its function? What does it plan to have it do?

The funny thing with the shadow government (if I may make an aside here, as I often do) is that now we are coming into the time of the absolute tyrannical rule, at least in the United States, though they will be mollified and modified somewhat in terms of what must be done internationally, you understand. The idea is to sort of snap the people of the United States to attention for a while and severely regulate them.

It's an odd thing; once you have placed a plan in motion, it moves under its own power and the people who are actually running, manipulating, setting policy for the shadow government, are already on the next phase and are totally disinterested. It's as if you were once thrilled about a project, but now you've got your managers and supervisors running it and you don't really care about it anymore. I mention that as an aside. What was your question?

They don't really care about what? The tyrannizing of the United States or the airplane?

Control by Medication

Tyrannizing the United States citizens in terms of regulation beyond —well, I can't say beyond your wildest dreams, but beyond some of our readers' and at least the wildest dreams of some of the people who don't read the magazine. People will very soon be encouraged to receive a medication that will be touted as the greatest genetic breakthrough for disease of all time. Now, I have to be careful what I say here because I do not want to discourage people from taking inoculations for diseases and so on, but you will have to be very careful when you talk to your doctor about what he is giving you.

You see, the government is going to begin touting a certain type of interferon, which is a drug, you understand, as the greatest cure for all disease. They will say it's a breakthrough, and so on. And it is a breakthrough in terms of its manufacture, because they can now manufacture it cheaply. But it is really something where the government will really have you if you take this intravenous injection. When they give you this injection, it really will cure or protect. It'll prevent, for certain, and in many cases cure, all known and unknown diseases that are currently epidemic or simply scattered here and there on Earth. And if you were exposed to a strange disease on the Moon or something, you would still be very resistant to becoming ill.

Now, you know, of course, that interferon is not permanent. You have to receive shots regularly. Perhaps the good type may be once a year; certainly at least with a weaker type, once every three months. Once you get the first shot, your immune system weakens by about 50%, because it's actually a form of synthetic immune system. Then as you continue getting your next shots, eventually you don't have an immune system at all. But if the shots are then stopped, the simplest little thing, even athlete's foot, could kill you because your immune system essentially is deprogrammed by your body's mechanism: "Oh, I'm not needed anymore. Well, goodbye, I'm out of here."

You have to be very careful now what they give the children in school. If they're going to have an injection program in school, be sure and ask what's being given. I'm not saying don't get shots for your children. A lot of those shots are good and they do help the children, although there is some valid argument that in the long run it depletes your immune system. But I don't want to open that can of worms. I will simply say this: Suppose they start giving that shot to your child. Then you find yourself in a position where you've got to get your child the next shot or he starts to get sick. You know what I'm saying? So they have you, you know, they've got you there.

There are a couple of new vaccines coming out. One will really be a good thing, but at least one or two others won't. One will be touted as a genetic cure. Watch out — it's true. It's a genetic cure; this is separate from the interferon. It's true that this genetic injection will strengthen you, *but it's also designed to alter the genetics of all people.* I don't feel good about that one, either, even though it will have some good side effects.

Alter how?

Well, it's actually designed to eliminate by natural selection, on a genetic level, the birth of children who have crippling diseases. You could say, "Wonderful. Then people who have some crippling disease running in their family and who can't have children can now have children safely." And I will say, yes. And you might say, "Oh, so if people who might otherwise have had a child that was born malformed or otherwise handicapped or challenged in life, that will not happen either." And I will say, "Most likely." But think how this could be used. This is another one of these things that is seductive on the surface. But I feel that in the long run genetic experiments are best left to the future, until, say, 35 years or so when you will all be significantly more spiritually advanced. Now, I know many of you are now advanced, but there are many who need to be. So I am putting in my two bits about waiting.

There will also be, not to be unkind to medicine, some new vaccinations that will do good things. So you just have to be careful. You need to be more informed with your physician, that's all. "What's in the shot? What exactly is that? How does that work?" Questions that most people do not ask their physician. And if the physician does not know, ask him or her to find out. Then you will all be informed.

I did not answer your original question here. Do you remember it?

The Use of the Light Ship

I asked what was the purpose, what was the shadow government going to do with this angelic craft? What was their purpose so that they would need to deceive the pilot, which would be impossible?

They originally intended to use this vehicle to escape the solar system. To travel far beyond, to (dare I say?) "go where no one has gone before." Their intended use was not to infringe on the copyright statement from Star Trek, but actually to seek out planets. This is a business, from their point of view, where mineral resources could be cultivated with a minimum of struggle — meaning, perhaps, planets where there are no occupants.

Life forms.

Life forms, of course. Or where suitable trade agreements could be set up to obtain strategic and other valuable materials. Of course, along the way if they discovered anything else useful or of value, they might find that worthwhile.

So they gave up trying to escape the solar system themselves and now they're just going to use it for exploration?

No. They're thinking in the long term of potentially colonizing someplace else that is more benevolent. You might live in St. Louis, Missouri, for instance, and drive out to the suburbs and find that you like it out there. So you move your family out into the suburbs while you continue to work in St. Louis. Using that analogy, they might continue to work on, around or near Earth and live someplace else. If you're traveling in Light, you might be able to easily live someplace else and just take a few weeks or so to get to work, as it were.

I'm not talking about the speed of light here, I'm talking about Light. This is a slightly different function from traveling in time. If you travel in the Light, you have the potential to meet Creator face to face. It's ironic: If you are shadow government people, you fear that, but on the other hand, you are drawn to it inexorably. So you hope maybe you will be able to negotiate with Creator. Because you know that no matter what you to do prolong your life, someday you will die and then you will have to negotiate. And I must say that regardless of all of the foundations and libraries and hospitals that have been built in the name of former robber barons and so on, after their lives were over, they found that when they talked to Creator, their negotiating power was considerably diminished compared to what they had when they were alive. Nevertheless, a good deed is always counted in your favor.

This is crazy. They were going to take this highly organized crime group, the ultimate in organized crime, and purify them — and now the angels are giving them Light ships so they can use it to tyrannize us? This is crazy.

Helping the Shadow Government
to Choose Transformation

No, no. Let's put it in a more microcosmic level. Let's say that you are dealing with an incorrigible murderer. How do you stop this person, short of killing them or strapping them down? You need to have these people change of their own free will to something that is of a higher, divine order. If you just come in and destroy their bodies —in other words, kill them —you have not changed them and they will still have to go someplace else to work out those unresolved emotions and feelings that have driven them into this life.

You said that they were going to get purified.

This is part of the purification. What happens if we give that murderer a fancy weapon and take him out and set him on Mars so he can shoot what he wants with it? There's nobody there to shoot physically, but the act of shooting feels good. Then he discovers that the act of just touching the weapon feels good, because it is a Light weapon, you see. You cannot use it without being transformed, and when you use it the transformation feels so good that you desire to have more of it. Since you understand how drugs work, at first you're afraid it's a drug, but then you realize that even if you don't have more of it, and discipline yourself not to do it, you feel fine, anyway. So you go back and have more. It transforms you.

My friend, I know I have stated that these people would be purified. If they can be purified and transformed while they are on Earth, it allows others whom they might affect after their physical life in incarnations elsewhere to be affected in a more benign way. It might allow them to become more benign. You must remember that uncreation and purification are rarely done. Allowance, pure allowance, and unconditional love require a desire by an individual to be redeemed.

So in a way, we use something that the shadow government uses itself. Shadow government has no compunctions about hooking people on addictive drugs of one form or another, whether it is disguised as something benign or simply for a thrill. If we do something like that with the shadow government itself, they will understand quickly. Might they not also become hooked on something that will uplift them? This is a mechanism of change.

Revenge just breeds more revenge. If we uncreate some being and take him back to the beginning of his creation, it means that some aspect of Creator is unfulfilled. It is hard for you to conceive that some aspect of Creator might be violent and destructive, and yet, is not Creator *all* things? If this is so, then how does that violent, destructive portion of Creator reach its fulfillment in order that it might be redeemed? Is it through killing, destroying? No. It is through discovering the value of unconditional love and allowance within one's self. How do you do that? You do it by giving it, but first you must receive it so you can realize there are no strings attached. I know how you are taking this, and you are right. Yet we are talking about personal, individual transformation as well as global, even galactic, transformation.

Violence = Extreme Impatience

Can you not imagine in the beginning of time when all things were equal and everything was vying for self-expression, how competitive the violent aspects were? Yet, before they learned to control through intimidation and destruction, they were not that way. The essence of the violent aspects is their impatient need to create. The essence of violence is extreme impatience. I know, the violent part is not funny, and yet the irony is that *impatience is at the core of all violence.* Even if impatience is not expressed, if it is there, it has the power and the ability to stimulate acts of violence, either toward oneself in the form of self-destruction, or to stimulate others who might be weathervanes for such acts, into violent acts they would not ordinarily commit were they living out in the countryside or the hinterland.

I am speaking to you today on the level of how creation is done. The shadow government must also be redeemed. We can give detail after detail of what they will or might do, and how they will manage to inject things into you that will transform you and make you dependent upon them, and how they will also put things inside you so that they will know everything about you, and all of these things we've talked about. And yet, do we not wish to redeem even the most violent sheep amongst us? How wonderful we all feel when that happens. This you understand very well.

Please ask about what you want to know.

I'm just trying to integrate all this. This is not the way I thought they played the game. It's like they're being helped to oppress and tyrannize.

Remember what I said at the beginning: One cannot fly this ship without being transformed. Suppose we send out the crew armed with guns, even ray guns. By the way, the government can have a working model of that in a year or so, and in two or three years, all of their forces will have a ray gun. Kind of puts bullets into the land of the archaic. This is not science fiction, this is real.

And the ray gun will do what?

If you point it at somebody, it will kill them. It is not a weapon of wounding as a bullet might be, provided you have a surgeon and a medical staff nearby. No, you just point it at someone, and zap, that's the end of them.

It can also be used even if people are in tanks. The ray gun may not destroy the tank, but it will create an energy inside that tank that will destroy any human being — which, by the way, is eventually going to lead to total automation of all armed forces. So you'll have tanks running around with no human beings inside. That's coming.

In our lifetime, in the next ten to twelve years?

Yes.

Well, who's on our side?

The angelic kingdom. And you must remember, now, what I said: You cannot fly these Light vehicles without becoming transformed. These men start out with these ray guns and they're going to go off to colonize or explore. Some of them are just scientists, not soldiers. They are not killers; they don't think of themselves that way. They are transformed. It is not possible to travel in a Light vehicle without being transformed. But the shadow government hopes that there is some way it can be done.

That they can travel without being transformed?

They think there's a way around it. Just so you will know that this is not the angelic kingdom defecting to the dark angel's side (well, that exists, but this is not that). These are golden beings. A long time ago, do you remember when it was spoken to you about how these wonderful beings of Light came and anointed the Orion warriors? Well, they have returned. There's your context. [See the book, *The Explorer Race,* by Zoosh through Robert Shapiro.]

That was the daughter of God, right?

Yes, and what would be called her servants, those who attend her.

I don't think I ever found out who she was. You called her the daughter of God.

Yes, but she didn't need a name. Names are for people who don't know who they are. Did you know that?

That's true.

Advanced Experimental and ET Craft

Tom called this morning and said that last night he saw two triangular UFOs go around Sedona three times. He said they flew right over, slow speed. Then there was another vehicle – he doesn't know if it was a plane or a UFO or what – that came from Flagstaff. It had huge flashing white lights followed by red lights. It went from north to south. Can you say what these are?

Again we're talking to some extent about shadow government experimental craft and to some extent military experimental craft. You know that your military has an advanced research project section and they are really somewhat unaware. The people who conduct and run the experimental services are actually the liaison between the shadow government vehicles as well as any other vehicles that might be here. The triangular vehicles are associated with the shadow government. They are not part of them, but they are an ally, or . . .

That's the Xpotaz.

There you are. They are people they would like to be allied with.

I thought that the shadow government had triangular UFOs.

They do, but you were asking about these two particular ships.

They were the Renegades. Okay.

Yes, and the vehicle following was a vehicle associated with the military advanced research project division

The one that came from north to south, right?

That's right. If you were to look at one of these vehicles, you could say that it looks somewhat like a jet plane when it's sitting on the ground. Yet it has the capacity to fly as a plane in absolute silence. Talk to some ranchers and people who live out in the countryside, and they will tell you they have seen these things flying overhead and they don't know what they are. Your government has these vehicles. That's part of the reason that the rest of the world tends not to press you for your debts. Because this plane is almost unstoppable. I'm going to call it a plane because I don't want to get it confused with something else.

Now, I know about these little red things. Those are from ET sources. Sometimes probes ranging from the size of a softball to a little smaller than a basketball might appear in those colors. A probe is essentially a surveillance vehicle, but it also has other capacities, which we've discussed. This one, however, was associated with an ET source that was monitoring the situation and has the capacity to travel intergalactically. It is specifically from a higher dimensional aspect of the Zeta Reticuli system. Joopah probably would know its exact intention.

But it was following those Renegade . . .

It was following everybody, kind of tagging along. They go where they wish to go. It's almost a struggle for them to travel so slowly.

But basically they're gathering information.

Yes. They gather information. They do not act on their own accord unless directed. They are fully automated.

And they're directed from this . . .

Higher-dimensional vehicle that is still nearby and which Joopah does interact with. This is a vehicle ranging in dimension from about the sixth to the seventh and can access anything below the seventh. Occasionally, in order to host Joopah, it can make momentary bursts to the ninth dimension, but does not maintain that. So when you see these little red things, they are usually something to enjoy. Know that they are definitely ET visitors, and, as I've said at length before, the Zetas are in your family. These things happen regularly now, and just about anybody can go out and look for these things. However, this man you have referred to [Tom Dongo] not only can see the physical, but he can also see the subtle because of his years of spiritual training. He might be able to see this, but there may be others who would not, even though they'd be standing right next to him. But it was a physical event.

Sedona's Position

Is Sedona sort of in the flight path, then?

You are now. That's part of the reason there's so much activity here. And also part of the reason, I might add, why there will be more in the future. I do not wish to discourage visitors to come to Sedona, because it is a place of great beauty, and yet *it may not be the idyllic small town that it once was* (in italics, if you would). It is also changing more and may even come a little quicker into the realm of control than is interposed in some bigger cities. Because Sedona is considered by those in certain legions (as in the Roman use of the term) to be, not government property, but like an extended base. So there is significant eavesdropping equipment in place activated in Sedona now.

But I thought the whole military, the whole shadow government, moved out. They're not in that base anymore.

They're not. But that does not mean that they do not wish to keep an eye on things. Sometimes you might go somewhere and not want to be seen, so you go back and brush out your tracks. If you are going somewhere, you tend to keep an eye on the rear as well as the front. That's why in the military they might have somebody on the point, but you would not forget to put someone in the rear so you can catch that person that might be sneaking up on you.

The last time we talked, there was hope that the ancient Pleiadian ship would talk the Renegades into leaving for more fertile pastures. What is the status right now?

These negotiations are ongoing, as negotiations usually are. Nevertheless, there is some hope for that. Because the Renegades really want, deep in their hearts, to go home — everybody does. Every single person, no matter what his orientation is, has a warm spot in his heart for home. Thus more than the Pleiadians are involved. The Renegades cannot go home because home isn't there anymore. How could it be created so home *could* be there? What is being negotiated through third- and fourth-party transactions is to literally recreate Xpotaz in some dimension that would allow these people to go home and have it feel like home to them, and to be provided with all they need to conduct a lifestyle that would support and nourish and nurture them. When you've been denied being able to go home ever again and can only do so in your memories or even in stories and tales that have been told to you, after a while you feel like you have less to lose than other people. There are motivations here that human people can understand. When you don't have much to lose because you can't go home, you are perhaps more prone to destructiveness.

What dimension would their home be?

To the Rengades, Home Is Stone

Probably it will be created in the second dimension, which will allow them to experience something that they miss dearly. That is the feeling of being a portion of rock or stone. These individuals were once a portion of a form of living stone in which they could go live inside the stone, though their bodies now do not really show that.

They miss this. It is like mother's milk, even more. It is like the heart of the Creator to them. If they can be provided this, even though they do not understand it in their current form, the minute they feel it they will know they are home. They will be safe, they will be protected. They will, of course, transform and no longer have a desire to be destructive to themselves or others. They will, in your current litany of liturgical terms, be SAVED (in capital letters).

But are you saying they would live in the rock and not come out?

They have a life in the rock. They would never come out. To you it would look like rock. And yet if you got up close to it, it would be hard to focus. You know, when you focus your eyes, you see clear, distinct lines. It would appear sort of blurry to you. Your hand would be clear and distinct, yet you would look at this "rock" and you would not be able to focus on it because it is living rock.

Now, I might add that this living rock has been seeded on Earth. What you see around you, these beautiful rock formations in Sedona and elsewhere, is actually living rock that has been seeded by people who grow rocks. This is not new. They are big only so that you will know that rock is alive. When people tear up rocks for their construction projects, they are not tearing up something inanimate. It is alive, but in that form. In this dimension it appears to be inanimate, but on second-dimensional Earth it is very much the same as Xpotaz, where it came from. So you see why the people of Xpotaz unconsciously, not even known to themselves, were drawn to Earth; there was something here that was like home.

Are you saying they came from our second-dimensional Earth?

No. Xpotaz is not your second-dimensional Earth. It is far, far away. And yet, on second-dimensional Earth, the rock is living. It is only in third dimension that it looks inanimate.

Is the second dimension interpenetrating, so if we could look second-dimensionally, we would see rock as living on third-dimensional Earth? Or would we have to go to the second-dimensional Earth?

You would have to go to second-dimensional Earth and you would have to be one of these people. If you are one of these people, or you have the ability to look with their senses and feel with their feelings, you would see it all. Those who are mystics on your planet can look into this native stone and see all the life within it.

Let's look at the probabilities. Are you going to transform the shadow government before they get the whole game played out? Are we going through this incredible control and being zapped or . . .

It will happen in a high-speed way. It was originally intended that the shadow government would take over and they'd be in control for ten thousand years or whatever. But it will not happen that long. I will say that by the experiential year 2017 you should notice that you yourself longer have any need or desire to control and that you feel much more patient — everyone will. When you never are motivated to control anything and are very patient all the time, you will know that the shadow government has been transformed.

Not long? I thought it was 2002.

Well, it takes time, does it not? You rush me all the time, you rush, rush, rush me.

Americans Are Expected to Sell Control

Is anyone going to step in and not allow them to . . .

You have been conditioned over the years. Right now Americans accept more control than most people in the world deal with, even in street signs and in driving, in getting this license and that license. You are so regulated that you will not feel the control as infringing on your rights that much, because your rights have been so infringed on already. It will take time to do it right. Let's do it right this time so we don't have to do it again.

As you're talking, I'm saying, why don't I just move to Tahiti or someplace? Is there a special purpose for those of us who are experiencing this control, because we have been the controllers? Is there a reason we need to stay here even though we know what's coming?

The shadow government intends to utilize the people of the United States as enforcers, as indoctrinary people. People of the United States are known throughout the world for being messianic, for telling how wonderful their system is, and their religion and their way of life, and wouldn't you (whether you live in Zaire or France or Brazil) like to have a way of life like ours? It is intended that the people of the United States become the agents, consciously or unconsciously, of the shadow government. That is why the propaganda machine is so mercurial and volatile here in the United States.

Contrary to what people feel, even though there will be travel restrictions for a short time, they will not last indefinitely, because it is intended that the people in the United States in their travels go out and say how wonderful it is in the United States and how we have this and that, and don't you wish you had that? You are intended to be the conscious, in some cases, but primarily unconscious, propagandists who will dampen the otherwise potent fueling of freedom of choice in other countries, especially those that have been dominated and controlled in recent years by powers such as Nazi Germany's control in France, where there are many people alive today who remember what that was like.

The Benevolent Resistance Movement

Fortunately, the French have an advantage because they are not easily controlled or manipulated or otherwise convinced. Oh, they might become silent, but that does not mean they are convinced. That nature is within them innately; it not only sometimes leads to their greatest errors, but inevitably leads to the benevolent resistance movement — BRM, as it will come to be called, at least privately. The benevolent resistance movement will gradually begin to spring up and even now is showing the tendrils of its manifestation in the form of political and environmental action groups geared toward the planet being allowed to be herself, and other aspects of what is called environmentalism. Not the politicized versions, but true environmentalism, the benevolent resistance movement, will spring forth from France and, believe it or not, Germany.

So then our role . . .

Your role is to become allies.

The role of people who read this? We're supposed to stay here and go through it?

It is up to them. If they wish to go to Canada, where they think it will be less extreme, by all means do so. Canada is involved, but the people there have a stronger sense of individual freedom and pursuit of their goals. They will not allow themselves to be as controlled, as manipulated, nor do they generally go out to the world and tell everyone that they must be like them. No, if they wish to escape this extremity, they can perhaps petition Canada for citizenship.

If citizens do not rise up and revolt when they read these things and many other writings that are being put out, equally volatile things, and state, "Look, here it is, this is going on," and there is no uprising or revolt, do you know why? There is one specific reason why.

Why?

Television. Television has become the addictive panacea. Not just what is said on television, the official news and so on, but what is done. Television is perhaps the most controlling, manipulating force in the United States that has ever existed. The rays that come out from the television screen alter your brain waves temporarily. People who watch, let's say, an average of four to six hours a day of television are not themselves. Take these people, put them out in the countryside where there is no television and where there is the least amount of microwave transmission, and they will become themselves again and have all of their creative impetus return. They will have ideas that stimulate them, but put them in front of television and their creative edge will be dulled. I might add that most successful executives and entrepreneurs know this, and that is why they do not watch television.

So people can stay here or leave.

The Safer Places

If people leave, they may find that it is best to move north. Generally speaking, the farther north you are, the safer you will be, with the possible exception of within three miles of the Canadian border. Right now the United States is building up their forces at the Mexican border, using the excuse of "too many Mexican people coming over to get jobs here." NAFTA is going to change that quite a bit. Eventually, as I've said (not so jokingly), U.S. citizens will be running across the border to get jobs in Mexico. Hard to believe, for those wages, and yet it will come. Within five years you'll probably start to see a buildup of forces, though not like the boundary between China and Russia years ago. You will see more so-called "border guards" there; at least people will believe that's what they are. You will also see some reaction on the Canadian side, because there will be some fear by that time from Canadian authorities that too many Americans are coming into Canada. Citizens of the United States will be coming into Canada to live there clandestinely without applying for citizenship, and you will see some reaction by the Canadian police forces, euphemistically referred to as the Mounties.

People might actually like being up in Montana. Why Montana? There's not that many people there. Montana is not going to like having all these people come, but they will get used to it. And they will see the bright side of it at some point. Though there will be some characters that you run into up there that you don't run into in Sedona, it will become known as the safe place.

Where in Montana?

Just about anywhere. Except you don't want to get within three miles of the border of Canada. It's true that there's a lot of rugged individuals there and a lot of people with serious ideas about things, but generally, these people all have one thing in common: a distrust of the government and support for individual rights of expression. So you might get some characters there who will put out some wild literature, but you will all have one thing in common, including yourself — a distrust of the government and a desire to see that things are returned to a position where people have individual rights.

This controlling element is going to increase, and some places you can live in the north and there will still be lots of control. But generally speaking, in what is now called the Southwest, there are few states that will be safer than others. Northern Idaho, Montana, Wyoming will be safer for quite a while, and northern Colorado. Let's see.

No place with sun and beaches?

Possibly. Oregon and Washington for a while yet. And then if things get to be a little congested, eastern Oregon and Washington. Let's see, most of northern Minnesota, most of North Dakota, some of South Dakota and most of northern Michigan. Yes, places that are known for their seasons, and in some senses for their extremes of weather. Yet it is those very seasons that renew and refresh. It is that cycle of renewal that creates a more benevolent state of being for Mother Earth.

Was there something that you wanted to say about this alien, ET shadow government?

The Crime and Health Bills

I think we've already covered it. Today I have talked about medical things because these things are relevant, part of your daily life now that the so-called crime bill has been passed. The purpose of the crime bill is to criminalize acts that are not criminal. It appears to be to control crime, but that is not true. It is really to criminalize things that are not criminal.

Give me an example.

Well, certain political activities will become criminal. Realize that I'm talking about people running for elective office. The bill can be interpreted that people who are going door to door will be somewhat restricted. Let's say you are running for city council. You can walk up to a door, knock on it in the evening hours (perhaps you have a job during the day) and say hello, and maybe the resident won't open the door because of fear or caution. And you say, "I am running for city council; may I speak with you? Here's my brochure," and slide it under the door. The crime bill can be interpreted to say that if anything is done (something shoved under the door without the owner's permission), it could be considered an invasive act. This is what is intended. I'm not saying this will be done, but the legal interpretation will be available.

It is actually intended to control political parties that are now coming up and getting going and building some momentum, such as the Libertarian party, which has been around for a while but is going to begin to look more attractive to many people. And also the new environmental party and other parties associated with specific causes. The Libertarian cause has always been for less government and more freedom, and that's going to look a lot more interesting to people. That's an example.

So it's going to give them more means to control people?

That's right. Watch out for the health bill, because that will be done there also. The crime bill created a federal police force. Certain federal authorities, whether they are these people or others, will, as a result of the health bill, be able to come around to a health practitioner's office, perhaps a chiropractor or a naturopathic physician or even a medical doctor and ask, "Do you have this license, do you have that license, have you been up to date in your licensing?" Everybody knows that physicians are usually up to date, and yet they do not always stay up to date with all of their reading and courses they must take to be completely aware of everything that's going on. Suppose a federal examiner comes into your office and asks, "Do you know this?" and it was printed in last month's Journal of the American Medical Association, and you as a physician, with all of the things you have to do and read, have not read this article. They ask you about it and you don't know the right answer and they say, "Well, your license is no good." The real underlying purpose — not the surface purpose, the benevolent purpose to provide health care to all people — of those who would put these bills through for their own reasons, is to further their control. Watch for that. It's going to be in the health care bill when it goes through.

To control practitioners?

That's right. And there is no stopping it. When you control the health care practitioners, you will control the people.

All right. I've got to absorb this one. This one is a biggie for me. This kind of goes against the way I think it should be.

You think of Creator and angelic or loving beings as following a certain path of love and support. But when there is a need to influence, a different approach must be used. This is something that Joan of Arc understood well. In order to be inspired, to be able to interact with those you wish to transform, very often you have to appear to them as someone they would admire, or at least fear with admiration. Do you know that Joan of Arc, as she is often pictured (though she did not look like that in her facial features, with the breastplate and so on), is very much the way the Orion warrior was described to you? The daughter of God and her beings of Light came from the Creator; they are all feminine, so that they will be polarized in love and nurturance. If you are going to transform someone who is a warrior, you must look like a warrior and have all the skills of a warrior so you can transform them in kind.

And this just occurred since the prime directive was recently rescinded? This is all just brand-new tactics?

That's right.

Well, bless you.

The Battle Begins

Jehovah through Arthur Fanning
September 23, 1994

Y ou're beginning to understand some of the things spoken of before, ages ago.

Yet still it is important to understand, regardless of this battle of Light going on, that you are who you are, that you are masters here, that is what you have come to understand. And if you don't get it, even though this process is going on, this battle, this great . . . from your prospective you would call it carnage. It doesn't matter because you are forever life. This is important. You are important individually in your Light. We'll get into the other thing here, this great controlling going on, this great fear. It is only fear that is doing this thing. You don't have the sides right, to begin with. That is all right, you will figure it out. There is this wave of Light beginning, and as this wave and this battle ensues, because you have your governments and they are playing picking sides, as usual, good/bad, you're going to be told which is the good side and which is the bad side. And it is only going to be the side that your controlling beings are on that they are going to say is good, you understand, unless you know who you are and your purpose, your Light Beingness here.

Now, I don't mean to make this sound like it is not a big deal; it is an outrageously big deal. Some of you are involved directly in the battle, some of you are not. But [it is] those of you that are, it is because you begin to understand who you are. Not that you've got it completely, but that you've got it a little bit and you still carry on some of the vestiges of this thought process here on your planet, what you term your fears, your doubts you play with. In *this* battle, there is not the slightest room for doubt of any kind to be involved here. Not at all.

Spiritual War Plan Complete by October 8

As these things accelerate, there is a planning stage going on now, a planning stage for what you would say the initial assault, and it is a little bit away, within what you would term your two weeks away. It'll be completed by what you would term the eighth of your October. Completed by what, I mean, I understand you to say, it would be planning complete for the assault. Know you that is the day we are doing this thing [all-day intensive]? And that is an important thing.

Now, your government is indeed going to begin to squeeze you, especially you in your metaphysical community, because you know too much. It won't bother you so much as you say, well, you play your little game; you'll be in the Light and be blessing all things. But they want to keep track of you in a manner that they can — and they have the ability to intercept you in your Lightbody to a certain extent, because of your belief systems. You beings haven't played out of your body enough to feel comfortable here, part of these things.

This war is a spiritual war in all aspects. Things will forever be changed upon your planet. We will not tell you the outcome because that will confuse you.

Lucifer is going to be involved here; [and] that is your name for this ancient being. Those that are of what you term the extraterrestrial origin, the limitations, the ravagers of peaceful beauty, so to speak, the rapers, have found themselves at a dead end in this thing. They want to switch sides now. Not going to be allowed.

Are these what we call the Xpotaz, the Renegade miners?

There are many. What you would term Renegades. There are many, there are many, know you?

So there are a lot more than just these 85 that we've been calling the Xpotaz, the ones who mine on the moon?

Indeed. You have other groupings coming from other systems also to get involved here. Beings are calling all their pieces together, like you here are too. They have many pieces.

It is going to be an outrageous display. The thing you must understand that when your sky Lights up and your daylight, you call it now — in your beautiful day, your sun, it is bright outside — it is going to become a thousand times more brighter that it is in your daylight. It will be a battle of the Light, within the Light, and the perception of those upon the planet will be that you are being attacked. But you're not being attacked. You're being what you would say protected. Not by your government at all.

Your government wants to control you, enslave you even more than you have been, and they are acting as defender of this place, indeed? For they are picking what you call an issue with the wrong beings. They think they have an understanding of the spiritual aspects of what you call the ability to move. This Light thing. But *behind* this spiritual understanding is a perversion, and that is where they have lost, do you understand?

As this battle ensues, becomes more, well, goes from skirmish to skirmish and becomes big grand conflagration. As it does, the aspects and play that you call time are going to change, shrink. They're going to be squeezed within time so that later, time won't exist. And that is a good thing, and that is a sad thing, for time is an outrageous playground. It won't exist here. It will be an end of certain fantasies, an end of certain structures that indeed provided a pleasant playground for a time, for a phase. But there is too much controlling going on now. It has gone out of hand, it has begun to affect what you term other systems in this energy, [that] you would term greed, and the energy you would term perversion of beauty. And that's why the great petition was made to higher, to the table before your Father, so to speak, and it was decided it is time to do it now. And that is beginning to happen.

The first scene, the first effect is going to be your government's, and another government's, movement upon this plane to demonstrate its power, to demonstrate its capacities, its abilities with these ships. And there'll be little bit of interfering there, likened unto a warning, "Don't do this any longer! Don't!" Know you? And they'll do it a little more, and we'll say, "Don't do this," and we'll take them down a little bit, shoot them, change them a little bit, and they'll still try to do, for they think they now have what you call a system that is powerful.

And after the third warning, then there will be called the twelve days of Light will begin to appear. Through all of this, mankind in its innocence is going to lose its innocence, and a majority, great number, will die from fear alone. Now you call play die, they are out of the body. And it is a not a judgment, that is the way the Light is going to be. We have told you about eating your fruits, indeed, because it allows the body physical form to vibrate very fast, and your vegetables also. And in that vibration you can hold more Light, and as you hold more Light, you're not affected in density by what you would term thought forms or the projections from these ships; you're not fooled. You understand. You don't begin to associate it with an aspect that, "Well, what can I do? I'm only a little being and you have this big government with all of these Neanderthals running around doing what they are told to do. How can I compete?" It is not a matter of competing on their level, it is a matter of you vibrating.

And then you will be vibrating at the same frequency of what you call their artilleries, so to speak, and they *can't* affect you. And you'll be vibrating at *least* enough so when the greater ships, this great armada, that come forth to change, to what you call correct the situation —your word correct — to balance. It will be likened unto friend coming home, because you are vibrating that fast you will understand it. If you're not vibrating that fast, you're only going to be able to understand, and the understanding is the knowing, and the knowing is the feeling within the being, within the body, of what the structures tell you. And sometimes what you see in front of your eyes is not the truth.

The Great Armada Is Coming

So it is a, one word you may say, a spiritual crisis for humanity. Many are going to say that this part of the war thing is Christ coming. Well, they've picked the wrong Christ on this one. The great armada will not appear right away. It is getting ready to be there. You're going to have your scout ships first to apply the warning, to apply the manipulation, to tell them not to do this thing. And we already know how that is going to work. And the great armada be coming.

Now, this armada, you could be standing upon your mountain and you will not begin to see where it begins nor ends. It covers galaxies; it is that much Light. But in what you call the human form here there are, well, you term your secret government, your shadow government, the beings that want to control this planet through their ability of their mind, what they call within the physical form human body, that have a system and developed a system of belief that they are gods, all-powerful here. And they are going to defy any other gods that are coming through to say they are not.

So they have, in a manner, this knowing, indeed, yet it hasn't been put to the test by them, so to speak, so they don't know, and it is a wrong test to play with the powers that are what will be termed most sacred, your word here, and that authority over all things, yet they be going to attempt it. Beings upon the planet, your human ones now, know this was going to happen, and you wanted to be here for the spectacle. Now you best understand this thing deep in your being.

There will be judgments within yourselves about which side you be choosing, but you must play in your Light. We've said this over and over and over. There are going to be plenty of opportunities to say bad guy, and obviously what is termed the bad guy is shadow government, that is the game they are playing now. They have never been the protectors of you, they've always been a manipulator and a grabber of your possessions. Going to be difficult for some to accept. You will accept it when your food supplies go away; you will understand that it is you alone walking upon the planet. It applies to each individual entity. There will be groupings, of course, and this is going to be a part of the awakening spiritually of humanity, and it is also going to be a part, indeed it is, when your localities, your areas, decide to be in their own spiritual travels, their own spiritual community. This is what is going to create the division, the breaking up of your state system here, your one thing.

Montana is already working on that.

There are going to be some political leaders that are going to have the courage to step forth in their glory, so to speak, to do this thing because they will understand, being politicians, that they are going to have to save their own hide, and that applies to these spiritual things that are going on now.

Now, what is part of this force, there are three armadas building here. They are awesome in their power and what would be termed all of your explosions that you've done on your planet, all of your bombs that you ever have used and the stockpile, etc. etc. do not even match what is termed a little bit, even what is termed a minuscule portion of the forces that they're going to be faced with. It be like a little firecracker compared to the power of these things. Now, life is a forever thing. It is this way, and that is what is going to assist human.

Altered Frequencies Create an Abyss

There is also this effect of these weapons that as you have built your body out of your thoughts and your belief systems and you live your life, so too you have built your spiritual forces around certain structures, certain frequencies. These ships be coming are going to alter those frequencies, and those beings that have held on to this system when the frequencies become altered will what is termed move, and have the effect to create an abyss, which is where they'll enter. Know you an abyss? That be called fear and doubt because they've only utilized one thing, their total obsession with greed and power.

And when that is altered, they will not go into a blast of Light and understand their glory, they'll go into the abyss, understanding their doubt of this greed and power, and it will last a long time. There will be many strange electrical storms upon your planet and they are created by the utilization of these weapons and the fact of the matter that the ships simply be flying in the arena. All of this is going to create turmoil and what would be termed turmoil, havoc, fear, and you're going to see your society, because you can't get together in a loving manner at any rate, that it is going to just accentuate the activity down here, and your government won't care, because they going to be too busy battling out there.

One of these things we've told you, these little ships going out to tell them "No, don't do that," it is to cool them off, to slow them down. "You don't really want to do this. It is not a wise thing." That activity is going to accelerate more and more.

When will it start?

The Collapse of Time

It has already started. All of this is leading up to the collapse of time, which in a manner is one of the things you beings wanted, in what you call the ascension, to blast into Light to understand. But you forgot how much fun time was here, and the reason it is leading into a collapse of time [is] because if they're allowed to succeed (they, being your shadow government, the beings that are controlling here), then you would be trapped forever in enslavement and it would spread. So as before, when you played with your tower of Babel, in your book, having wars with the gods, so too you are going to do it again. You should have taken some advice from that piece of literature. It didn't succeed that time. It won't succeed now, either.

So that was a similar situation with the beings who controlled the planet; Light forces were brought in? It wasn't just that the languages were separated? It was another air war like this?

It was, indeed.

But it's much older than the Bible — when was it, actually?

Very long time ago in a manner. How would we say — it is a myth and in reality it occurred in another place, not this place, you understand? And this place was created for those beings to come to evolve beyond that thing, and the myth was brought here.

From Orion?

It had to do *with* Orion, not from that portion. The system no longer exists.

There is a possibility but . . . and it hasn't been decided yet, in a manner; it is still being discussed . . . that we take this ship out of operation immediately. And it is also a possibility that we'll petition more for beings to come home, drag them out of their bodies, so to speak.

The Secret Government's Light Ship

Can you amplify that? I don't understand. There is a possibility you would take what ship away from the secret government?

This Light ship they be playing with.

This new Light ship that was on the evening news? Why was it given to them?

It was sort of, we'll say, I know you say given; it was they finally figured out how to apply some spiritual power, know you, and then they went crazy with it. Do you understand? So, in a manner, it has taken what you would term, some beings you term masters, to begin to function here, and power, and has a great energy thing. You must understand these beings must do this thing, that is what they are driven by, you understand, driven by the need for power. So they sort of, we'll put it this way: It wasn't kept from them. Once they have a certain level of spiritual understanding, then it is available. So it wasn't given, per se, likened unto "Here is a gift." It was given in a manner that they have applied some force, and, still driven by their power, it was allowed to be, to see what they would do with their power. Now, in a manner you can be say that would be given, and the extraterrestrials, because they found themselves involved with what you call this Light coming forth, figured they still have a chance, know you, of defeating the Light. Well, it isn't going to happen.

All right. I heard from Zoosh that the angelics gave it to them to transform them on the planet rather than to purify them, and I got real upset about that.

It be likened unto this. As they become more spiritually aware, indeed, they be allowed to have access to this information, do you understand. And so it was available, and they utilized it. Yet being driven so much by their power, because they need to understand power, they have taken it to use it as a weapon. So in a manner what is termed Zoosh is correct. It was given by the angelics to see and hope that they would utilize it purposefully. And because of their of their power and their desire for this thing, it was perverted again, indeed. Yet they must truly be in their ignorance and arrogance, because that was already anticipated, do you understand? They could go off the deep end with this thing we were aware.

We allowed choice here to be important, and we also have many scenarios playing out here as you play your time-shrink. You have heard of this thing called the battle of Light coming for many years now, indeed, and it is what was foreseen. It was because of man's arrogance and his spiritual ignorance, we had a pretty good idea of the tendencies and the avenues that were going to be taken with choices, and you're pretty well following schedule. That is because you put your power into the other beings that you call your government.

You don't need to be governed, by the way. You need to be allowed to live. That is allowing you to live. You have your priorities all mucked up. That is all right. You beings want a show, and we have told you this before easy, it is going to be a great play for you to watch, and you're all part of it. That's why it is important for you to be into your arena. Now, as this moves — and I said earlier, we can say you at this time, call them forth, call all of their Light back out — but this time we must allow some level of, what do you term, the ability to redeem themselves. So we offer and offer this thing, you term it redemption, as to understand love, more and more we offer until it is going to be finished.

So it is not going to play out until 2002, then, or is it?

It is speeding up. You are all getting involved in it, and your year 1995 is going to be very emotional, very intense in this arena, and that is simply the beginning. Your year what is termed your 1997 will be in the manner, the way it appears now, the great one, the great conflagration, and then we will stabilize through your year 2002 and it will be completed. But you're heading into this finality aspect in your 1997.

Conflagration — are you saying that the cities are going to burn, something like that?

More than your cities, your souls will burn, out of fear. It is not something you want to think is a game, yet it is in greater understanding, but your arrogance is going to tell you it is different. And everyone will be affected everyone.

And time will start shrinking when, in '97? It's been shrinking, but it is going to speed up shrinking?

It will indeed speed up, shrinking towards your '97.

Well, this is the end of the book, Volume One, so . . .

It is the beginning of a book.

Well, it is the ending of this particular little one.

The wars haven't truly begun yet, yet they have. There are only little skirmishes going on now. And the big one is coming.

Zoosh said the beings up here now, the billions of them from everywhere that are doing the technical stuff, don't fight because they are in their Christ consciousness, and they had to go back half a million years to get these Pleiadian warriors. If that is so, then who is coming in these armadas who can fight? Are all of these beings going to change now, or how does that work?

The Ancient Pleiadians, the Initial Assault Forces

Well, it won't . . . there are a lot of the Pleiadians here, and it is a good thing for you that they are, because of the structure.

The ancient ones or the modern ones?

The ancient ones.

They are the ones who blew up the underground base in Sedona, right?

They are. They are the ones that be the initial frontal assault, you would say, from this . . . frontal is not the right word. The initial assault forces to provide warnings.

Is it possible that they are past lives of any of us? Or we're not connected?

It is that they are integrating a lot of their energies into this time, this thing. Now, the other beings of Light that you say are in their Christ consciousness, they are beyond their Christ consciousness.

Well, okay, but they don't fight, they allow?

They don't have to fight because they are, and what you don't understand are thoughts. They understand to think a thing or not think a thing is the creation of it or not. Do you understand? And they are allowing these things to happen. That's going to be one of the weapons. Because when you come through on this side of the hole, if we declared that this ship didn't exist, and didn't allow it in the thought, it wouldn't [exist]. Do you understand? "It is not a battle for us, it doesn't exist!" From your perspective it would be a battle.

But that's the beings from beyond the black hole [the galactic core].

They are coming through in this armada.

All right!! But the other beings around the Earth now, the scientists and technocrats, those from Arcturus, Andromeda and Zeta Reticulum — beings from this galaxy — don't normally fight, do they? Isn't that why they had to go back to get the ancient Pleiadians?

That is true, on this side. But you're forgetting the ones coming through the hole.

That's wonderful. I hadn't known they were coming.

You'll wish they never experienced these ones.

The secret government will wish that.

And many others.

So the lines will be drawn. They will either be on the side of greed and power and corruption, or of humanity. How does it work out with humanity? A politician could seek greed and power or he could be trying to serve. How is this going to split humanity?

Don't be so much inclined with their words; be inclined with their actions and their feelings, know you. In this time it is a time for masters, and *masters* are going to have difficulty walking upon this planet in this time.

Why are they going to have difficulty?

Not only are you moving beyond the what you call you say you be a master, you be a Christ or you be the Buddha. As you begin to understand more, you've got to go beyond the Christ and beyond the Buddha. So those that are finally beginning to get their Christhood and play and do a little bit of manifestation . . .

If they stick there, they're going to have trouble if they don't go beyond that.

Indeed. We're getting into the *real* nitty gritty now, and you must go beyond the Brotherhood of Light. You be there with them as they go through their little confrontations.

Who are they going to confront?

They're confronting your secret government. These are ones you don't want to mess with, either. They have an attitude [he laughs].

Are there higher parts of any of us involved in this war?

Indeed. You're all out there at certain levels of activity.

This is the end of our book. Is there anything else you want to say?

That will be all for now.

BOOK MARKET

*A reader's guide to the extraordinary books we
publish, print and market for your enLightenment.*

COLOR MEDICINE
The Secrets of Color Vibrational Healing
by **Charles Klotsche**

A practitioners' manual for restoring blocked energy to the body systems and organs with specific color wavelengths by the founder of "The 49th Vibrational Technique."

$11.95 Softcover 114 pp.   ISBN 0-929385-27-6

THE STORY OF THE PEOPLE
by **Eileen Rota**

An exciting history of our coming to Earth, our traditions, our choices and the coming changes, it can be viewed as a metaphysical adventure, science fiction or the epic of all of us brave enough to know the truth. Beautifully written and illustrated.

$11.95 Softcover 209 pp.   ISBN 0-929385-51-9

THE NEW AGE PRIMER
Spiritual Tools for Awakening

A guidebook to the changing reality, it is an overview of the concepts and techniques of mastery by authorities in their fields. Explores reincarnation, belief systems and transformative tools from astrology to crystals and healing.

$11.95 Softcover 206 pp.   ISBN 0-929385-48-9

THE SEDONA VORTEX GUIDEBOOK
by **12 various channels**

200-plus pages of channeled, never-before published information on the vortex energies of Sedona and the techniques to enable you to use the vortexes as multidimensional portals to time, space and other realities.

$14.95 Softcover 236 pp.   ISBN 0-929385-25-X

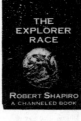

COMING SOON!

THE EXPLORER RACE
A channeled book
by **Robert Shapiro**

In this expansive overview, Zoosh explains, "You are the Explorer Race. Learn about your journey before coming to this Earth, your evolution here and what lies ahead." Topics range from ETs and UFOs to relationships.

BEHOLD A PALE HORSE
by **Bill Cooper**

Former U.S. Naval Intelligence Briefing Team Member reveals information kept secret by our government since the 1940s. UFOs, the J.F.K. assassination, the Secret Government, the war on drugs and more by the world's leading expert on UFOs.

$25.00 Softcover 500 pp.   ISBN 0-929385-22-5

NEW!

THE COMPLETE ASCENSION MANUAL
How to Achieve Ascension in This Lifetime
by **Joshua David Stone, Ph.D.**

An overview of the teachings of the spiritual Hierarchy —the 7 levels of initiation, with a main focus on how to achieve ascension in this lifetime. Fascinating insights and techniques.

$14.95 Softcover 242 pp.   ISBN 0-929385-55-1

LIVING RAINBOWS
by **Gabriel H. Bain**

A fascinating "how-to" manual to make experiencing human, astral, animal and plant auras an everyday event. Series of techniques, exercises and illustrations guide the simply curious to see and hear aural energy. Spiral-bound workbook format.

$14.95 Softcover   ISBN 0-929385-42-X

TALKS WITH JONATHON
Book 1
As told to **Robin Miller**

The limited past perception of what is real and unreal is soon to be altered. With clarity and compassion, Jonathon sets forth guidelines for those on the path of self mastery in this changing time.

$14.95 Softcover 160 pp.   ISBN 1-81343-04-9

BOOK MARKET

EXPLORING LIFE'S LAST FRONTIER

by

Dr. Heather Anne Harder

By becoming familiar with death, the amount of fear and grief will be reduced, making the transition and transformation of Earth more joyful. A manual for learning acceptance and letting go.

$15.95 Softcover 315 pp.   ISBN 1-881343-03-0

REIKI A TORCH IN DAYLIGHT

by

Karyn K. Mitchell

An inspiring guide to clarify the Usui Method of Natural Healing, the book presents a step-by-step vision of the origins and techniques for teachers and students. Complete with detailed illustrations and photos, it is a powerful training.

$14.95 Softcover 153 pp.   ISBN 0-9640822-1-7

NEW!
LIFE ON THE CUTTING EDGE

by

Sal Rachelle

To explore some of the most significant questions of our time requires a cosmic view of reality. From the evolution of consciousness, dimensions and ETs to the New World Order, this is a no-nonsense book from behind, about and beyond the scenes. A must-read!

$14.95 Softcover 336 pp.   ISBN 0-9640535-0-0

BOOKS BY VYWAMUS / JANET MCCLURE

FOREVER YOUNG

by

Gladys Iris Clark

You can create a longer younger life!

Viewing a lifetime of nearly a century, a remarkable woman shares her secrets for longevity and rejuvenation. A manual for all ages. She explores the tools for optimizing vitality, nutrition, skin care, Tibetan exercises, crystals, sex and earth changes. A fascinating guide to transforming.

$9.95 Softcover 109 pp.   ISBN 0-929385-53-5

SANAT KUMARA Training a Planetary Logos

Vywamus
through
Janet McClure

How was the beauty of this world created? The answer is in the story of the evolution of Earth's Logos, the great being whose name is Sanat Kumara. A journey through his eyes as he learns the real-life lessons of training along the path of mastery.

$11.95 Softcover 179 pp.   ISBN 0-929385-17-9

THE SOURCE ADVENTURE

Vywamus
through
Janet McClure

Life is discovery, and this book is a journey of discovery "...to learn, to grow, to recognize the opportunities—to be aware." It asks the big question, "Why are you here?" and leads the reader to examine the most significant questions of a lifetime.

$11.95 Softcover 157 pp.   ISBN 0-929385-06-3

AHA! THE REALIZATION BOOK

Vywamus
through
Janet McClure
with Lillian Harben

If you are mirroring your life in a way that is not desirable, this book can help you locate murky areas and make them "suddenly...crystal clear." Readers will find it an exciting step-by-step path to changing and evolving lives.

$11.95 Softcover 120pp.   ISBN 0-929385-14-4

LIGHT TECHNIQUES THAT TRIGGER TRANSFORMATION

Vywamus
through
Janet McClure

Expanding the Heart Center... Launching Your Light... Releasing .. Weaving the Garment of Light...Light Alignment and more. A wonderfully effective tool for using Light to transcend and create life as a Light being. Beautiful guidance!

$11.95 Softcover 145 pp.   ISBN 0-929385-00-4

SCOPES OF DIMENSIONS

Vywamus
through
Janet McClure

Vywamus explains the process of exploring and experiencing the dimensions. He teaches an integrated way to utilize the combined strengths of each dimension. It is a how-to guidebook for living in the multidimensional reality that is our true evolutionary path.

$11.95 Softcover 176 pp.   ISBN 0-929385-09-8

BOOK MARKET

BOOKS BY TOM DONGO

NEW!
UNSEEN BEINGS UNSEEN WORLDS
by **Tom Dongo**
Venture into unknown realms with a leading researcher. Discover new information on how to communicate with nonphysical beings, aliens, ghosts, wee people and the Gray zone. Many photos to depict ET activity and interaction with humans.

$9.95 Softcover 122 pp.   ISBN 0-9622748-3-6

THE QUEST
The Mysteries of Sedona III
by **Tom Dongo**
Fascinating in-depth interviews with 26 who have answered the call to Sedona and speak of their spiritual experiences. Explores the mystique of the area and effect the quests have had on individual lives. Photos/illustrations.

$8.95 Softcover 144 pp.   ISBN 0-9622748-2-8

OUT-OF-BODY EXPLORATION
A Guide to New Dimensions of Self-realization
by **Jerry Mulvin**
Techniques for traveling in the Soul Body to achieve absolute freedom and experience truth for oneself,. Discover reincarnation, karma and your personal spiritual path.

$8.95 Softcover   ISBN 0-941464-01-6

THE ALIEN TIDE
The Mysteries of Sedona II
by **Tom Dongo**
The UFO and ET events and paranormal activity in the Sedona area and nationwide are investigated and detailed by a leading researcher who cautions against fear of the alien presence. Intriguing information for all who seek new insights. Photos/illustrations.

$7.95 Softcover 128 pp.   ISBN 0-9622748-1-X

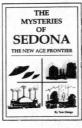

THE MYSTERIES OF SEDONA
by **Tom Dongo**
An overview of the New Age Mecca that is Sedona, Arizona. Topics are the famous energy vortexes, UFOs, channeling, Lemuria, metaphysical and mystical experiences and area paranormal activity. Photos/illustrations.

$6.95 Softcover 84 pp.   ISBN 0-96227480-0-1

THE GOLDEN PATH
Channeled by **Ruth Ryden**
"Book of Lessons" by the master teachers explaining the process of channeling. Akashic Records, karma, opening the third eye, the ego and the meaning of Bible stories. It is a master class for opening your personal pathway.

$11.95 Softcover 200 pp.   ISBN 0-929385-43-8

BOOKS BY WES BATEMAN

COMING!
THE RODS OF AMON RA
by **Wes Bateman**
Space Age mathematics – an integrating theory of the physical universe revealing God in matter. Extraordinary information, includes over-size charts and data.

$49.95 Softcover   ISBN 0-929385-60-8

KNOWLEDGE FROM THE STARS
by **Wes Bateman**
A telepath with contact to ETs, Bateman has provided a wide spectrum of scientific information. A fascinating compilation of articles surveying the Federation, ETs, evolution and the trading houses, all part of the true history of the galaxy.

$11.95 Softcover 171 pp.   ISBN 0-929385-39-X

DRAGONS AND CHARIOTS
by **Wes Bateman**
An explanation of spacecraft, propulsion systems, gravity, the Dragon, manipulated Light and interstellar and intergalactic motherships by a renowned telepath who details specific technological information he has been given through contact with ETs.

$9.95 Softcover 65 pp.   ISBN 0-929385-45-4

BOOK MARKET

BOOKS BY PRESTON B. NICOLS/PETER MOON

THE MONTAUK PROJECT
Experiments in Time
by **Preston B. Nichols** with **Peter Moon**

The truth about time that reads like science fiction! Secret research with invisibility experiments that culminated at Montauk, tapping the powers of creation and manipulating time itself. Exposé by the technical director.

$15.95 Softcover 160 pp. ISBN 0-9631889-0-9

MONTAUK REVISITED
Adventures in Synchronicity
by **Preston B. Nichols** with **Peter Moon**

The sequel unmasks the occult forces that were behind the technology of Montauk and the incredible characters associated with it.

$19.95 Softcover 249 pp. ISBN 0-9631889-1-7

MAHATMA I & II
Brian Grattan

Combined version of the original two books. Guidance to reach an evolutionary level of integration for conscious ascension. Fascinating diagrams, meditation conversations.

$19.95 Softcover 328 pp. ISBN 0-929385-46-

ACUPRESSURE FOR THE SOUL
by **Nancy Fallon, Ph.D.**

A revolutionary vision of emotions as sources of power, rocket fuel for fulfilling our purpose. A formula for awakening transformation with 12 beautiful illustrations.

$11.95 Softcover 150 pp. ISBN 0-929385-49-7

SOUL RECOVERY & EXTRACTION
by **Ai Gvhdi Waya**

Soul recovery is about regaining the pieces of one's spirit that have been trapped, lost or stolen either by another person or through a traumatic incident that has occurred in one's life.

$9.95 Softcover 74 pp. ISBN 0-9634662-3-2

I'M O.K.
I'm Just Mutating!
by **the Golden Star Alliance**

Major shifts are now taking place upon this planet. It is mutating into a Body of Light, as are all the beings who have chosen to be here at this time. A view of what is happening and the mutational symptoms you may be experiencing.

$6.00 Softcover 32 pp.

AN ASCENSION HANDBOOK
by **Serapis** through **Tony Stubbs**

A practical "how-to" guide for Lightworkers for increasing the frequency of energy bodies to emerge as self-realized Masters. Ascend with grace, ease and fun.

$11.95 Softcover 140 pp. ISBN 0-880666-08-1

E.T. 101:
COSMIC INSTRUCTION MANUAL
Emergency Remedial Edition,
Co-created by **Mission Control** and **Diana Luppi**

A witty guide for evolving beyond the programming and manipulation.

$12.95 Softcover 86 pp. ISBN 0-9626958-0-7

OUR COSMIC ANCESTORS
by **Maurice Chatelain**

A former NASA expert documents evidence left in codes inscribed on ancient monuments pointing to the existence of an advanced prehistoric civilization regularly visited (and technologically assisted) by ET's.

$9.95 Softcover 213 pp. ISBN 0-929686-00

BOOKS BY LYNN BUESS

CHILDREN OF LIGHT: CHILDREN OF DENIAL
by **Lynn Buess M.A., Ed.S.**

In his fourth book Lynn calls upon his decades of practice as counselor and psychotherapist to explore the relationship between karma and the new insights from ACOA/ Co-dependency writings.

$8.95 Softcover 150 pp. ISBN 0-929385-15-2

NUMEROLOGY: NUANCES IN RELATIONSHIPS
by **Lynn Buess M.A., Ed.S.**

Provides valuable assistance in the quest to better understand compatibilities and conflicts with a significant other. A handy guide for calculating your/his/her personality numbers.

$12.65 Softcover 239 pp. ISBN 0-929385-23-3

NUMEROLOGY FOR THE NEW AGE
by **Lynn Buess M.A., Ed.S.**

An established standard, explicating for contemporary readers the ancient art and science of symbol, cycle, and vibration. Provides insights into the patterns of our personal lives. Includes life and Personality Numbers.

$9.85 Softcover 262 pp. ISBN 0-929385-3

BOOK MARKET

BOOKS BY ELWOOD BABBITT

PERFECT HEALTH
by **Elwood Babbitt**

For the first time ever, the world's most respected names in medicine and science speak through the noted trance medium. Wilhelm Reich, Einstein and others offer opinions on AIDS, nutrition, Life purpose.

$15.95 Softcover 297 pp.   ISBN 1-881343-01-4

VOICES OF SPIRIT
by **Elwood Babbitt** and **Charles H. Hapgood**

The author discusses 15 years of work with Elwood Babbitt. This book will fascinate both the curious skeptic and the believer. Includes complete transcripts.

$13.00 Softcover 350 pp.   ISBN 1-881343-00-6

PRISONERS OF EARTH
Psychic Possession and Its Release
by **Aloa Starr**

The symptoms, causes and release techniques in a documented exploration by a practitioner. A fascinating study that de-mystifies possession.

$11.95 Softcover 179 pp.   ISBN 0-929385-37-3

BOOKS BY RICHARD DANNELLEY

THE SEDONA UFO CONNECTION
And Planetary Ascension Guide
by **Richard Dannelley**

A history of humanity's involvement with aliens from ancient times, it explains how we have been helped, hindered and how we can protect ourselves from alien interference with evolution.

$11.95 Softcover 128 pp.   ISBN 0-9629453-0-7

SEDONA POWER SPOT, Vortex and Medicine Wheel Guide
by **Richard Dannelley**

An exploration of the vortex legends and their effects on the mind and spirit. Meditations, maps and photographs to guide the reader to profound transformation.

$9.95 Softcover   ISBN 0-9629453-2-3

THIS WORLD & THE NEXT ONE
by **Aiello**

A handbook about your life before birth and your life after death, it explains the "how" and "why" of experiences with space people and dimensions. Man in his many forms is a "puppet on the stage of creation."

$9.95 Softcover 213 pp.   ISBN 0-929385-44-6

BOOKS BY ROYAL/PRIEST

PRISM OF LYRA
by **Lyssa Royal & Keith Priest**

Traces the inception of the human race back to Lyra, where the original expansion of the duality was begun, to be finally integrated on earth. Fascinating channeled information.

$11.95 Softcover 112 pp.   ISBN 0-9631320-0-8

VISITORS FROM WITHIN
by **Lyssa Royal & Keith Priest**

Explores the extraterrestrial contact and abduction phenomenon in a unique and intriguing way. Narrative, precisely focussed channeling & firsthand accounts.

$12.95 Softcover 171 pp.   ISBN 0-9631320-1-6

PREPARING FOR CONTACT
by **Lyssa Royal & Keith Priest**

Contact requires a metamorphosis of consciousness since it involves two species who meet on the next step of evolution. A channeled guidebook to ready us for that transformation., it is engrossing.

$12.95 Softcover 188 pp.   ISBN 0-9631320-2-4

BOOKS BY DOROTHY ROEDER

THE NEXT DIMENSION IS LOVE
Ranoash through **Dorothy Roeder**

As speaker for a civilization whose species is more advanced, the entity describes the help they offer humanity by clearing the DNA. An exciting vision of our possibilities and future.

$11.95 Softcover 148 pp.   ISBN 0-929385-50-0

REACH FOR US
Your Cosmic Teachers and Friends
Channeled by **Dorothy Roeder**

Messages from Teachers, Ascended Masters and the Space Command explain the role they play in bringing the Divine Plan to the earth now!

$13.00 Softcover 168 pp.   ISBN 0-929385-25-X

COMING SOON!
CRYSTAL CO-CREATORS
Channeled by **Dorothy Roeder**

A fascinating exploration of 100 forms of crystals, describing specific uses and their purpose, from the spiritual to the cellular, as agents of change. It clarifies the role of crystals in our awakening.

$11.95 Softcover   ISBN 0-929385-40-3

BOOK&TAPE MARKET

B O O K   M A R K E T   O R D E R   F O R M

BOOKS PUBLISHED BY LIGHT TECHNOLOGY PUBLISHING

		NO. COPIES	TOTAL			NO. COPIES	TOTAL
ACUPRESSURE FOR SOUL *Fallon*	$11.95	___	$_____	SOUL REMEMBERS *Warter*	$12.00	___	$_____
ALIEN PRESENCE *Ananda*	$19.95	___	$_____	SOULS, EVOLUTION and the FATHER *Fanning*	$12.95	___	$_____
BEHOLD A PALE HORSE *Cooper*	$25.00	___	$_____	STORY OF THE PEOPLE *Rota*	$11.95	___	$_____
CHANNELLING: Evolutionary Exercises *Vywamus/Burns*	$9.95	___	$_____	THIS WORLD AND NEXT ONE "Aiello"	$9.95	___	$_____
COLOR MEDICINE *Klotsche*	$11.95	___	$_____	***Wesley H. Bateman***			
COMPLETE ASCENSION MANUAL *Stone*	$14.95	___	$_____	RODS OF AMON RA–I	$49.95	___	$_____
I AM VICTORY *Busse*	$10.95	___	$_____	DRAGONS AND CHARIOTS	$9.95	___	$_____
EXPLORER RACE *Shapiro*	$24.95	___	$_____	KNOWLEDGE from the STARS	$11.95	___	$_____
FOREVER YOUNG *Clark*	$9.95	___	$_____	***Lynn Buess***			
GOLDEN PATH *Ryden*	$11.95	___	$_____	CHILDREN OF LIGHT...	$8.95	___	$_____
LIVING RAINBOWS *Bain*	$14.95	___	$_____	NUMEROLOGY: Nuances	$12.65	___	$_____
MAHATMA I & II *Grattan*	$19.95	___	$_____	NUMEROLOGY for the NEW AGE	$9.85	___	$_____
NEW AGE PRIMER	$11.95	___	$_____	***Dorothy Roeder***			
PRINCIPLES TO REMEMBER *Maile*	$11.95	___	$_____	CRYSTAL CO-CREATORS	$11.95	___	$_____
PRISONERS OF EARTH *Starr*	$11.95	___	$_____	NEXT DIMENSION IS LOVE	$11.95	___	$_____
SHINING THE LIGHT	$12.95	___	$_____	REACH FOR US	$13.00	___	$_____
SEDONA VORTEX GUIDE BOOK	$14.95	___	$_____	***Vywamus/Janet Mcclure***			
SHADOW OF S.F. PEAKS *Bader*	$9.95	___	$_____	AHA! THE REALIZATION BOOK	$11.95	___	$_____
				LIGHT TECHNIQUES	$11.95	___	$_____
				SANAT KUMARA	$11.95	___	$_____
				SCOPES OF DIMENSIONS	$11.95	___	$_____
				THE SOURCE ADVENTURE	$11.95	___	$_____

BOOKS PRINTED OR MARKETED BY LIGHT TECHNOLOGY PUBLISHING

		NO. COPIES	TOTAL			NO. COPIES	TOTAL
ASCENSION HANDBOOK *Stubbs*	$11.95	___	$_____	***Elwood Babbitt***			
DEDICATED TO SOUL *Vosacek*	$9.95	___	$_____	PERFECT HEALTH	$15.95	___	$_____
E.T. 101 INSTRUCTION MANUAL *Mission Control/Luppi*	$12.95	___	$_____	VOICES OF SPIRIT	$13.00	___	$_____
EXPLORING LIFE'S... *Harder*	$15.95	___	$_____	***Richard Dannelley***			
HOOPS ACROSS AMERICA *Sarki*	$12.95	___	$_____	SEDONA POWER SPOT/GUIDE	$9.95	___	$_____
"I'M OK..." *Golden Star Alliance*	$6.00	___	$_____	SEDONA UFO CONNECTION	$11.95	___	$_____
LIFE ON CUTTING EDGE *Rachelle*	$14.95	___	$_____	***Tom Dongo: Mysteries of Sedona***			
OUR COSMIC ANCESTORS *Chatelaine*	$9.95	___	$_____	MYSTERIES OF SEDONA—Book I	$6.95	___	$_____
OUT OF BODY EXPLORATION *Mulvin*	$8.95	___	$_____	ALIEN TIDE—Book II	$7.95	___	$_____
REIKI *Mitchell*	$14.95	___	$_____	QUEST—Book III	$8.95	___	$_____
SOUL RECOVERY/EXTRACTION *Waya*	$9.95	___	$_____	UNSEEN BEINGS...	$9.95	___	$_____
TALKS WITH JONATHON *Miller*	$14.95	___	$_____	***Preston B. Nichols with Peter Moon***			
TAPESTRY OF LIGHT *Drew*	$11.95	___	$_____	MONTAUK PROJECT	$15.95	___	$_____
THE ARMSTRONG REPORT *Armstrong*	$11.95	___	$_____	MONTAUK REVISITED	$19.95	___	$_____
				Lyssa Royal and Keith Priest			
				PREPARING FOR CONTACT	$12.95	___	$_____
				PRISM OF LYRA	$11.95	___	$_____
				VISITORS FROM WITHIN	$12.95	___	$_____

ASCENSION MEDITATION TAPES

		NO. COPIES	TOTAL			NO. COPIES	TOTAL
Vywamus/Barbara Burns				***YHWH/Arthur Fanning***			
THE QUANTUM MECHANICAL YOU	(Set of 4) $40.00	___	_____	ON BECOMING	$10.00	___	_____
Brian Grattan				HEALING MEDITATIONS/ KNOWING SELF	$10.00	___	_____
EASTER SEMINAR RESURRECTION—1994	(Set of 6) $59.95	___	_____	MANIFESTATION & ALIGNMENT WITH POLES	$10.00	___	_____

**BOOKSTORE
DISCOUNTS
HONORED**

SEND ☐ CHECK OR ☐ MONEY ORDER
(U.S. FUNDS ONLY) PAYABLE TO:
**LIGHT TECHNOLOGY
PUBLISHING**
P.O. BOX 1526 • SEDONA • AZ 86339
(602) 282-6523 FAX: (602) 282-4130

NAME/COMPANY_____

ADDRESS_____

CITY/STATE/ZIP_____

PHONE_____CONTACT_____

All prices in US$. Higher in Canada and Europe.

SUBTOTAL: $_____

SALES TAX: $_____
(7.5% – AZ residents only)

SHIPPING/HANDLING: $_____
('3 Min.; 10% of orders over '30)

CANADA S/H: $_____
(20% of order)

TOTAL AMOUNT ENCLOSED: $_____

CANADA: Cherev Canada, Inc. 1(800) 263-2408 FAX (519) 986-3103 • ENGLAND/EUROPE: Windrush Press Ltd. 0608 652012/652025 FAX 0608 65212

We will continue to
"Shine the Light of Truth"
on this magical, multidimensional
"reality" we create and inhabit.

Watch for future installments
in the *SEDONA Journal of EMERGENCE!*
and in the ongoing
Shining the Light series of books.